D0914601

# EDITING NINETEENTH-CENTURY FICTION

# Conference on Editorial Problems

## Previous Conference Publications

The Conference volume for 1978 will deal with the editing of letters and will be edited by Alan Dainard.

# EDITING NINETEENTH-CENTURY FICTION

Papers given at the thirteenth annual
Conference on Editorial Problems,
University of Toronto,
4–5 November 1977

## EDITED BY JANE MILLGATE

*Garland Publishing, Inc., New York & London*

*1978*

Library of Congress Cataloging in Publication Data

Conference on Editorial Problems, 13th, University
   of Toronto, 1977.
   Editing nineteenth-century fiction.

   Includes index.
   1. Editing--Congresses.   2. Fiction--19th century--
Congresses.  I. Millgate, Jane.  II. Title.
PN162.C62  1977             801'.95             78-3393
   ISBN 0-8240-2428-1

Printed in the United States of America

# Contents

# Notes on Contributors

SYLVÈRE MONOD is Professor of English at the University of Paris. He is the author of *Dickens Romancier* (1953; translated as *Dickens the Novelist,* 1968), *Charles Dickens* (1959), *Histoire de la littérature anglaise de Victoria à Elisabeth II* (1970), and *Histoire du roman anglais* (forthcoming), and the editor and translator of six novels and two volumes of tales in the Pléiade edition of Dickens, of which he is now General Editor; he has translated other novels, including *Wuthering Heights* and *Jane Eyre,* and is also General Editor of the Pléiade Conrad. With George H. Ford he has edited two Dickens novels for the Norton Critical series: *Hard Times* (1966) and *Bleak House* (1977).

PETER SHILLINGSBURG is Associate Professor of English at Mississippi State University. He is the author of articles on editing and on Victorian literature and General Editor of a new edition of the Works of Thackeray which is currently in preparation and in which his own edition of *Pendennis* will appear. He edited the special Thackeray volume of *Costerus* (1974) and served in 1976-77 as Coordinator of the Modern Language Association's Center for Scholarly Editions.

MICHAEL MILLGATE is Professor of English at the University of Toronto. He is the author of *William Faulkner* (1961), *American Social Fiction* (1964), *The Achievement of William*

*Faulkner* (1966), *Thomas Hardy: His Career as a Novelist* (1971), and of numerous articles on English and American literature. He has edited works by Tennyson, Dreiser, Faulkner (with James B. Meriwether), and Gosse (with Paul F. Mattheisen). He is currently engaged (with Richard L. Purdy) in editing for the Clarendon Press *The Collected Letters of Thomas Hardy,* of which the first volume was published in 1978, and in writing a biography of Thomas Hardy.

CLIVE THOMSON is Research Fellow of the Zola Research Centre at the University of Toronto and a member of the team currently editing *La Correspondance d'Emile Zola,* the first volume of which will be published by the Presses de l'Université de Montréal in 1978. Dr Thomson is the author of critical and textual papers on Zola, and has completed an édition critique of *Paris.*

HERSHEL PARKER is Professor of English at the University of Southern California. He is Associate Editor of the North-western-Newberry edition of *The Writings of Herman Melville,* for which he has edited (with Harrison Hayford and G. Thomas Tanselle) *Typee* (1968), *Omoo* (1968), *Redburn* (1969), *Mardi* (1970), *White-Jacket* (1970), *Pierre* (1971), *Moby-Dick* (forthcoming), and *The Confidence-Man* (forthcoming). In addition to numerous articles on American literature and on editing, Professor Parker has published *The Recognition of Herman Melville* (1967) and edited the Norton Critical editions of *Moby-Dick* (1967, with Harrison Hayford) and *The Confidence-Man* (1971).

JANE MILLGATE is Professor of English at the University of Toronto. She is author of *Macaulay* (1972) and of critical and textual articles on Scott, Charlotte Bronte, Thackeray, Macaulay, and others, and is currently writing a critical study of Sir Walter Scott. She acted as convenor of the Conference on Editing Nineteenth-Century Fiction and has edited the present volume.

# EDITING NINETEENTH-CENTURY FICTION

# Introduction

# Jane Millgate

The thirteenth annual Conference on Editorial Problems, held at the University of Toronto on 4 and 5 November 1977, focused on the editing of nineteenth-century fiction. Four of the papers were devoted to single authors — Dickens, Thackeray, Hardy, and Zola — while the fifth took its principal examples from Hawthorne, Mark Twain, and Stephen Crane. The range of works from English, American, and French literature was wide in itself, and it became clear early in the Conference, from the discussion that followed the papers as much as from the papers themselves, that different scholars had different attitudes towards the editorial process and very different ambitions for the texts they were seeking to produce.

Sylvère Monod, for example, in his uniquely difficult and responsible role not only as editor but as translator-editor, was especially concerned with the need to make texts fully accessible to readers of different cultural backgrounds, and laid a particular stress, therefore, on the problems of annotation. Peter Shillingsburg, believing that Thackeray's post-publication revisions served to diminish rather than enhance his work, sought to recover for the modern reader a closer approximation to the experience of Thackeray's contemporary readers — to present the novels as they stood at the time of first publication, or as they would have stood had Thackeray's intentions of that date been ideally realized. Hershel Parker was similarly convinced that an author's final intentions were not necessarily the best, but his conclusion was not that first intentions should automatically be followed in their stead but rather that the editor, in making his decisions, should draw not only upon bibliographical and biographical evidence but upon the resources of literary theory and of other related disciplines. Clive Thomson proved to be fascinated by the genetic process itself and even speculated upon the possibility of rendering typographically the successive stages of textual transmission; not surprisingly, he wanted textual and historical introductions placed at the front of editions and not at the back, as has become customary in recent American publications. Michael Millgate spoke essentially as an historian of the text, seeking to demonstrate that any editor — whatever his ultimate decisions — must first accumulate all possible evidence that could conceivably throw light on the transmission process; while he, too, acknowledged that an author's revisions might occasionally seem aesthetically dubious he nevertheless insisted upon the dangers involved, at least in a Hardy text, in setting the editor's judgment above the author's.

There has for some time been ample evidence of a reaction against the sheer massiveness of the editions prepared under the auspices of the Center for Editions of American Authors and against the principles vaguely — often all too vaguely — associated with that composite ogre known as "Greg-Bowers." The revolt was perhaps inevitable, and it has at least been useful in gaining general acceptance for the idea — partly anticipated in Bowers's own comments on "practical" editions — that there is a place for texts prepared for many different purposes and on many different principles, so long as those purposes are clearly perceived and the principles clearly spelled out. The case for or against extensive annotation, for example, can scarcely be argued on general grounds but only in terms of a particular text intended for a particular audience. Nor could there be any objection, in principle, to an attempt to demonstrate by some system of symbols the sequence of pre-textual forms; there are, after all, advantages to the standard British (and especially Clarendon Press) procedure of giving textual variants at the foot of the page, and one could imagine an editor primarily interested in the "avant-texte" going so far as to adapt to published work some version of the "inclusive" format normally reserved for previously unpublished materials such as notebooks or journals. On the other hand, the tendency of such an edition might well be to emphasize the descriptive and analytical introductory material at the expense of the text itself — to such a point that the latter was abandoned and the intro-duction developed into a book-length genetic study published on its own terms.

The case for presenting texts that directly reflect a particular moment not only in the author's development but in the larger pattern of literary history is also an attractive one. It ought surely to trouble the literary scholar that while he thinks and writes of a particular novel as belonging peculiarly to the date at which it was first published, the text he has in his hand is likely to have been significantly affected by the subsequent intervention of the revising author, an older and in some ways a different person — Peter Shillingsburg, for example, insisted that the man who revised *Pendennis* was better off and on better terms with the world than the man who wrote it. Clearly, an editor, after examining all the relevant evidence, might well argue successfully for the

superiority of an early state of the text in question: Hershel
Parker has supplied some graphic demonstrations of what an
author is capable of doing to his own work, and I have myself
suggested elsewhere that some of Scott's revisions in the 1830
text of *The Bride of Lammermoor* succeeded in correcting a
particular historical error only at the expense of impairing
the historicity of the work as a whole, so that an editor of
that novel might wish to follow the original readings of at
least those particular passages. It goes almost without saying,
however, that such a claim could only be firmly established
by the inclusion within the apparatus of evidence (e.g., collation tables) covering all forms of the text, late as well as
early, in which the author might have had a hand. Failing
such documentation the sense of historical authenticity
might be better recaptured simply by the publication of
facsimile reprints of first editions, enhanced as necessary by
appropriate introductory material: a good many texts of
this kind have already appeared, of course, and for the
nineteenth century they have proved especially useful when
the illustrations formed an essential part of the original
experience — as in Mark Twain's *A Connecticut Yankee,*
published in facsimile by Chandler some years ago.

None of these possibilities, however, would seem to render
inevitable or desirable the demise of the kind of authoritative
edition represented by, for instance, the Ohio State Hawthorne
and the Northwestern-Newberry Melville. No one now
seriously claims absolute "definitiveness" for such editions,
and it is perhaps time that the term was abandoned even as
a convenient Aunt Sally; on the other hand, it is worth
keeping in mind the extent to which the massive scholarship
involved in their preparation has been ultimately dedicated to
the purpose — very American in its democratic idealism — of
making available to scholar, student, and common reader
alike the best single text obtainable by the combination of
rigorous scholarship with critical acumen, and of doing so in

a *clear* text, undisturbed on the page by editorial interventions of any kind, and thus readily separable from the scholarly apparatus and potentially available for reproduction in a cheaper format. It is, of course, true that this idealism has rarely proved realizable in practice — often for practical reasons for which the editors themselves cannot be held responsible — but even if few paperback issues of the texts of the CEAA editions have as yet appeared it is not clear that the idea has lost its validity. Professor Todd Bender was cited by Peter Shillingsburg as insisting that there are many different states of any particular work and that each of these has its own validity, but while that may be true — it is, after all, implicit in the standard editorial search for all potentially relevant forms — it does not necessarily take us very far, except in terms of those potential scholarly uses of computers to which Professor Bender was chiefly addressing himself: the decisions about the actual text to be printed in the main body of any edition remain. The assumptions and practices of editors must change, and are changing, as more is learned about editing and, often as a result of editorial endeavours, about the creative process itself. But the concept of the authoritative edition, aimed at bringing all available knowledge to bear upon the production of a widely usable text, is unlikely to lose its importance, whatever other types of edition may appear to fill particular scholarly or popular needs. What emerged sharply from the 1977 Toronto Conference, however, was the equal unlikelihood of the debates about editing losing their vitality: in particular, the debate about authorial intentions, and the nature of the editor's responsibility in determining and observing such intentions, is only in its early stages and will be sustained for some years to come, certainly in print and no doubt in the papers and discussions of future Toronto conferences.

As convenor of the thirteenth Conference it remains for me to extend the grateful thanks of the Committee of the

Conference on Editorial Problems to the Canada Council for its generous financial support, to the University of Toronto for sponsoring the Conference, and to the Master of Massey College for welcoming the participants to the College. I would like also to express my personal thanks to the other members of the Conference Committee, especially Alan Dainard, Hugo de Quehen, Francess Halpenny, J. R. de J. Jackson, Anne Lancashire, and Desmond Neill; to Kinny Kreiswirth for designing the Conference poster; to Elizabeth Hulse and Richard Landon for mounting in the Thomas Fisher Rare Book Library a special exhibition on Nineteenth-Century Fiction and producing the accompanying catalogue; to Michael Collie and George H. Ford for chairing sessions of the Conference; to Carolynn Jackson for setting the text of this volume; and to Tara Ghoshal for assistance with the proofs.

# "Between Two Worlds": Editing Dickens

## Sylvère Monod

When I confess that I come before you today "fresh from the horrors my own hands have made," you may not identify this phrase as a Dickens quotation. Yet it is one; it is not spoken by my favourite character in my favourite Dickens novel. In fact, the speaker is Mr Rudge senior, Barnaby's father, who is denied the right to a first name or even an initial, as part of the punishment of his many crimes, no doubt; well, this gentleman relates how, just after committing two murders, he presented himself before his wife, "fresh from the horrors my own hands had made." I have not committed two murders, or even one, but I have perpetrated two editions of *Bleak House,* one American, the other French, and they both entered the final stages of publication in 1977. That is surely an unusual position, it is even to a certain extent a privileged one, and I think I may take advantage of it and give you the benefit of that twofold and twice hard-earned expertise.

One of the editions is, like a previous *Hard Times,* the product of close collaboration with Professor George Ford for the Norton Critical Editions series; the other, begun under the general editorship of Pierre Leyris for the Bibliothèque de la Pléiade in Paris, was completed with myself as both captain and crew, and this volume will be eked out by the *Christmas Stories.* My expertise is thus international and bilingual. I live "between two worlds" myself. But the difference between other editors of Dickens and myself in that respect is one of degree, not of kind. We all have the same job, which is to make our author *genuinely accessible;* both these words are important; it is not enough to provide a genuine text, or the best possible text, we must also make that text accessible. And we can never take it for granted that there is only one best text: our prospective and implied readers may well have specific needs and demands.

Being French and working on French editions of Dickens increases one's awareness of the fact that editing involves more than textual work. The needs of a French reader are not identical with those of a British reader, and both are distinct from those of a North American reader. In each country there are several classes of readers, from general public to students to scholars and experts.

Even in textual matters proper, policies have to be chosen with a view to the implied reader. Editors do not work in a vacuum, since they have been commissioned by a publisher for a series which has its rules and principles depending on the potential market — that is, after all, on the implied purchaser. Editors have no right to despise the publisher's commercial preoccupations, which are intrinsically legitimate and largely coincidental with the editors' interests; but perhaps editors should insist on having their own way if their suggestions are likely to make it easier for people not merely to purchase the book, but to use it. All editorial decisions have to be made for the benefit of implied readers.

But I have said more than enough of generalities. I can now more usefully devote myself to the problems involved in editing Dickens, and first of all to the textual side. In the middle 1960s, the idea of textual work on Dickens' novels finally ceased to appear eccentric. Already in 1959, John Butt had put forward his sensible "Proposals for an Edition of Dickens"[1] which later formed the basis of the policy followed by the Clarendon Dickens. The Clarendon *Oliver Twist* and the Norton *Hard Times* appeared in 1966, a year after John Butt's tragically premature death. The three Clarendon and the two Norton volumes are so far the only critical editions of Dickens novels to have been printed anywhere.

The Dickens editor has an abundance of material at his disposal on the textual side, especially when tackling one of the eight or nine long novels originally published in monthly instalments. For each of these the textual materials available normally include: a set of memoranda or working notes and plans used by the author; a complete original manuscript; at least one set of proofs corrected by Dickens, and in some cases two or even three successive sets; a first edition in parts or in one volume; three further editions published in the author's lifetime. These basic facts are so well known that it may be superfluous to review them once more; yet they form the groundwork of many of my illustrations. Likewise, a word must be said about the ever astonishing fact that for his monthly novels Dickens was committed to providing each month exactly thirty-two pages of print of exactly fifty lines each; it is unnecessary to point out here the aesthetic implications and consequences of such a procedure, but it is clear that there were practical consequences also, such as the need to trim the number to size at proof-stage, whenever it was not miraculously just right, that is, when there were two pages too many or twenty lines too few; this inevitably influenced the very nature of Dickens' work as a proofreader.

But while we have every reason to be grateful to Dickens himself, to his executor John Forster and to the Victoria and Albert Museum in South Kensington for preserving and gradually making more and more accessible so many documents of immense value to the textual editor, we also have every reason to deplore that there are gaps in our knowledge of the textual history of a Dickens novel. I shall mention three of them briefly at this point: we do not know what was the exact purpose or function of those memoranda, or "mems", as Dickens himself called them; they would seem, on the face of it, to have been mainly prospective, that is, concerned with the planning ahead of a novel in progress; but there are signs that the mems also had a retrospective or recording function. Then, it is good to have proofs corrected in Dickens' own hand, but it is not good enough, for there are many passages where changes have been made between manuscript and the earliest set of proofs we have, or between two existing sets of proof, or between the latest set to have been preserved and the text of the first edition. Similarly, we lack information as to the nature and extent of Dickens' work on the preparation of the so-called "Charles Dickens Edition," the latest to have been sanctioned by him, and thus the one that would be recommended as copy-text by a certain loudly authoritative school of textual criticism.

Let us examine the editor's tasks, difficulties, and problems when faced by the elements at his disposal in the editing of a Dickens novel.

The memoranda or "mems" are undoubtedly of considerable interest. Since they were first discovered — not that they had ever been concealed or buried, but for sixty or seventy years no one cared for them — they have been commented on, extracted from, reproduced in facsimile or in legible transcriptions, in short exploited in almost every possible way. I suppose no serious editor nowadays would regard a new *Bleak House* as worth its salt, or simply as complete, without a full set of mems appended to it. Two questions arise in connection with them, however: one is, can the mems stand on their own legs (spindly as they are) or should they be reinforced and illuminated by commentary, however conjectural? And are they to be given in facsimile or in printed transcription or in some kind of compromise between the two? The disadvantage of a facsimile is that it is often illegible, except to the trained eye of the near-professional Dickens editor (and no editor is proof against misreadings of the mems — or of the manuscript); the disadvantage of the printed transcription is that it gives only a faint idea of what the mems actually look like: for instance, there are all kinds of squiggles and underscorings of varying thickness, energy, or colour; the variations presumably mean something, or express some intention. I do not have the answer to these queries; I can only say that on the second point I personally regard a compromise between the two extremes as less unsatisfactory than anything else: the actual wording of the mems made readable, and the lines, tickings, underscorings, etc., suggested to the reader. I would also say that, having provided readers with these materials, we should leave them to interpret them in their own way, rather than force upon them our own interpretation.

The original manuscript of a Dickens novel poses gigantic problems. No one, as far as I know, has yet suggested that one of them would be worth printing complete in facsimile, all six or seven hundred crowded pages of it. Editors will probably long be left to the solitary enjoyment of poring over these opaque scrawls and scribbles. I am not going to describe a Dickens MS in detail — though that is one of my favourite themes, about which I tend to sound self-pitying — but I must mention a major textual editorial problem connected with it: the question of size. I mean that no one has tried hitherto, that perhaps no one will ever try to decipher and record the thousands of erasures in a Dickens manuscript, though they unquestionably form part of the textual history of a novel; perhaps they could be salvaged by using the techniques of infra-red photography; but most of us have to work with microfilms of the manuscripts, and it is not at all certain that all the erasures could eventually be read, and in any case there is a staggering number of them. One has to become resigned to the fact that any novel, and especially a Victorian three-decker, is considerably longer than a sonnet or even a five-act play, where every word, every letter almost, of every stage of the textual history can be amorously identified.

The corrected proofs are fascinating and rewarding documents; to the same degree as the mems and the original manuscript they give us a picture of Dickens at work on the text of his novels; they deserve to be very carefully examined and to have their items recorded in the textual notes of a serious edition (but, for obvious reasons, probably not reinserted within the text itself). The nature and sometimes the purposes of changes introduced by Dickens at proofstage are discernible; in addition, one can see that Dickens was both tried and tired by the time he reached the end of a novel: the final chapters of *Bleak House* show him to have become a less efficient proofreader than he had been in the earlier phases of the same book. And, presumably like most authors, he tended to relax after he had caught and corrected one or more bad mistakes in a paragraph, so that he would then let one or more others subsist.

The question of a copy-text is one of the vexed issues of textual editing. The two extreme theories, both vigorously defended by their respective champions, are that the only allowable copy-text is the manuscript when that is available, or, conversely, that the only allowable copy-text is the latest edition sanctioned by the author. But neither of these is

satisfactory in the case of Dickens' novels: the manuscript,
as I said before, is for one thing far from clear; for another,
it is sometimes faulty in little matters of spelling or word-
order and the like; and it is gravely deficient in punctuation,
since Dickens liked to introduce his own — highly idiosyn-
cratic — system of punctuation mainly at proofstage. The
latest edition published in Dickens' lifetime and sanctioned
by him is of course the Charles Dickens Edition of the late
1860s; but there is no evidence that Dickens did any work
on the text for that edition, apart from writing running head-
lines for the first time; there is no certainty, in the case of
*Bleak House,* that a single change for the better was deliberately introduced into that edition by the author; there is
abundant evidence that it incorporates all the mistakes that
had crept into the intermediate editions (the Cheap and
Library Editions) and coins a considerable number of fresh
mistakes. The process that leads from the 1853 edition of
*Bleak House* to all the current editions available nowadays is
one of steady deterioration, since they are all based on the
Charles Dickens Edition and usually preserve all its errors,
not without adding to the number. So that the best possible
copy-text — such is my belated conviction — is the first
edition in volume form, which is remarkably free from
misprints, even without taking into consideration the frantic
haste with which it was prepared.

The popular reprints, like the Riverside in the United
States and the Everyman's Library in Britain, have typically
adopted the Charles Dickens Edition text and contributed
a new batch of misprints. It is only recently that textual
interest has resulted in the appearance of better texts and
more considerate choices. The Clarendon novels began with
a strong bias in favour of the Charles Dickens Edition, but
have moved away from that position reluctantly, though
perceptibly. Our first Norton Critical Edition (of *Hard Times*)
laboured under the same delusion; but the Clarendon and

Norton editors at least attempted to use all the other available forms of the text to modify and improve the Charles Dickens version; not so some volumes in a very — and on the whole justly — popular British series, where it is claimed at best that the mistakes of the Charles Dickens Edition have been silently corrected; that is simply not true, except in the case of the few that could be easily identified without going through the harrowing process of a word by word comparison with the 1853 text of *Bleak House,* for instance; so that the British paperback edition I am referring to, though it has an excellent introduction and very useful explanatory notes (and full transcriptions of the mems) is textually meaningless. Another *Bleak House* published in paperback by a respectable American firm makes a wiser choice of basic copy-text in selecting the 1853 first edition, but is perhaps less than wise in deciding to reproduce it warts and all — that is, with all of the few original misprints reverently emulated. To be precise, that edition reproduces as many of the original mistakes as the compositors have been persuaded to keep; but compositors are "contrairy" creatures; they will be lavish of misprints when you wish to get a clean text; but when you want them to commit misprints, they will discover that their professional pride is at stake; they will find it beyond their powers to print "counsinship," and thus make the footnote "thus in 1853" nugatory when it is attached to the word "cousinship"; and perhaps the compositors' instinct is right, on the whole; for the interest of perpetuating such over-sights is minimal, except to the antiquarian.

Indeed, a good edition of *Bleak House* in my opinion is one that follows the best text ever printed, but improves it by borrowing, not freely, but judiciously, from earlier stages of its history (such as the original manuscript) as well as from later versions, the rule being that in every case the editors aim at the text that Dickens himself would have approved. As I said before, there is not much advantage in adhering to the

Charles Dickens Edition, though it provides a certain amount of normalization in spelling, punctuation, hyphenation, capitalization, etc., that was carried out with the author's at least tacit acceptance. I fail to see what rule of sound editorship might preclude our taking advantage of such changes. In the other direction — that is, in retrieving manuscript readings ignored by the compositors and not restored by Dickens while proofreading — a policy of infinite prudence must be worked out, for this lends itself to much controversy. A manuscript reading may be retrieved only when both the internal and the external evidence point that way; the internal evidence lies in the greater adequacy of the manuscript form, in its making obviously much better sense, or much better English; the external evidence is to be found in the difficulties of the manuscript, in the fact that it was understandably misleading, because of a misplaced or ambiguous caret mark, for instance, and also in the proliferation of corrected mistakes around the uncorrected one. A manuscript reading cannot be restored, however great the temptation may be, unless there is definite proof that it was indeed disregarded by both compositor and proofreader; it cannot be restored if it occurs in the same chapter as even one other departure from manuscript introduced on a missing set of first proof. To make this point, which is to me of vital interest, clearer, I would like to refer to specific incidents in the textual history of *Bleak House*.

In that novel, Dickens had to correct scores of blatant misreadings of his manuscript that resulted in things like "Dip me" for "Pity me," "winking" for "walking," and "of her penalty" for "of her presently." In each of the "bad" chapters of *Bleak House*, there could be as many as forty of these misreadings, and Dickens' failure to correct some of them is pardonable. The consequences, however, are unfortunate. An interesting example is provided by Chapter V ("A Morning Adventure"); Mr Jarndyce's wards are taken by Miss Flite to old Krook's shop. Krook is much attracted by the beauty of Ada's hair, and says, in every edition of the novel ever printed: "Hi! Here's lovely hair! I have got three sacks of ladies' hair below, but none so beautiful and fine as this." Going back to the corrected proofs, of which there are two sets, we find that the first set read "Here's lovely hair! Strong hair! I have got three sacks of etc." In the printed version there is some abruptness in the passage from the exclamation to the assertion. Something to fill in a probable gap and serve as a transition would be very welcome. But not "Strong hair!" which is hardly an improvement. On going back one further step, however, one can just decipher on the manuscript the intelligible and intelligent transition it did provide. For what Dickens had originally written was: "Here's lovely hair! I buy hair! I have got three sacks of etc." The words "I buy hair!" were inserted in exceptionally tiny writing above the line. Only a trained reader of Dickens' manuscripts can make anything of them. Obviously the compositor couldn't. And when Dickens read his proofs, one of two things must have happened: either he did not have his manuscript at hand, or he could not read what he had written. In any case, he cancelled the stupid misreading "Strong hair!" but failed to restore the missing link "I buy hair!" He may have been in a tremendous hurry. But he ought to have realized that compositors invent nothing, that "Strong hair!" had not been engendered by spontaneous creation. But the fact is that he didn't, or behaved as though he didn't. And therefore we — the Norton editors — did not feel justified in retrieving that particular manuscript reading; I would very much have liked to do so; I am not far from considering that the intrinsically commonplace statement "I buy hair!" is one of the very best things in *Bleak House*. But the evidence is clearly before us: Dickens decided that after all nothing was needed between "Lovely hair" and "I have three sacks." That was a mistake, a wrong decision, but we have no right to be kinder to Dickens than he is to himself. We might have tried to persuade ourselves that Dickens had been interrupted just as he was about to restore "I buy hair" after cancelling "Strong hair" and forgot to complete the substitution after the interruption had come to an end. But that is pure conjecture. There is not one scrap of evidence that way. All we know is that Dickens appears to have read a second set of proofs and still left things as they were.

I have discussed that example at some length because it is amusing, but mainly because it illustrates the extreme prudence with which these matters have been dealt with in our edition of *Bleak House.* We have in fact made over a hundred retrievals, but we have tried never to take undue liberties.

Not that we can claim our edition will be a textual model. It infringes some of the theoretical rules by not recording all accidentals, by not giving lists of divided words, etc. It omits some variants because it does not aim at being perfect in the abstract, but at being useful; our rule has been on the whole to record only such variants as offer interest of some kind and actually reveal something about the history of the text, Dickens' methods of work, and the processes of his artistic creation. Our choices and exclusions have been conditioned in part by the size of the task, in part by our understanding of our implied readers. We decided, for instance, that their appetite for accidentals would be satisfied, or satiated, by one specimen chapter in which all variants, including spelling, punctuation, hyphenation, are recorded; for Chapter V, therefore, our edition has 186 textual notes. For the whole volume, not quite four thousand. Admittedly, this leaves out a large number of divergences between the various states of the text which were recorded in my private notes but did not find their way into the edition; or at least they are not listed individually, but they are mentioned in a fairly elaborate general note on the text. Admittedly, also, part of our problem was one of space; a one-volume *Bleak House* which includes backgrounds, bibliography, a sampling of contemporary and later criticism, cannot indulge itself in a lavish or luxurious critical apparatus. In other words, while our reader could be kept comfortably implied, our publisher was very concretely real and present, looking over our shoulders, over the four shoulders that, like Mr Vholes in the novel, we had put to the wheel.

Most of the compositors' misreadings have been left out, when they were corrected by Dickens, because they are not part of the creative process through which the present state of the text came into being.

I seem to be explaining that we have excluded from our textual notes almost everything. That is not the case, since we have, not quite, but very nearly, four thousand recorded variants. They include a few manuscript peculiarities, all words and passages cancelled or inserted at proofstage, and all substantive variants in the three later editions.

Examples, once more, will perhaps be more telling than general descriptions. I shall take them mainly from the first ten chapters. The careful reader — when she or he ceases to be merely implied, we like to think the reader will turn out to be interested and attentive — will find quite a number of puzzles, not discussed by us, but embedded in the textual notes. For instance, one occurs in Chapter V, when Esther and her party, emerging from Mrs Jellyby's house, meet "the cook round the corner coming out of a public-house, wiping her mouth." Why did Dickens, at proofstage, cancel one detail, i.e., that the cook originally came out of the public-house with a hackney-coachman? Did he belatedly regard this allusion as improper and fear to call a blush to the cheek of the young person? But that is in a novel whose heroine was born of the criminal amours of a penniless officer (a penniful officer would be far less shocking) and the future Lady Dedlock. And in any case it is not at all improper, but on the contrary quite proper that any servant of such a mistress as Mrs Jellyby should be addicted to hackney-coachmen as well as to pints.

Textual work, as I have already shown in the case of the hair-purchasing business, has its temptations. I have also shown why I think they ought to be resisted. Here are other examples, from the very beginning of the novel, from that famous first paragraph, which is a translator's nightmare and touchstone. Of Chapter I, there is evidence that the missing first set of proofs included several significant cancellations. The temptation would be to deny this and to feel that one is enriching one of the finest pages Dickens ever wrote by adding to it, for instance, after "Fog up the river, where it flows among green aits and meadows" those splendid words "full sponges at present from which the hop of a sparrow would squeeze out superabundant moisture," or a little later, after "the gas . . . has a haggard and unwilling look," the no less memorable and characteristic sentences: "Nothing has any defined outline. Passengers, vehicles, horses, and houses, all ghosts together." Textual editing demands enormous powers of self-denial and rigorous honesty. Relegating such splendours to the dim half-light of the textual notes is heart-rending (you will notice that by mentioning them here I draw attention to them and thus pour balm on my own heart), but it is inevitable, for that kind of omission does not occur by accident where the manuscript is relatively clear. But the reasons for the cancellations are certainly worth investigating. The textual annotation does no more and no less than its proper job by providing the materials in the rough, and leaving the reader to "piece out our" — and Dickens' — "imperfections with their thoughts."

Textual notes will also supply evidence of the way in which the text has steadily deteriorated from one edition to the next, and most spectacularly in the much vaunted Charles Dickens Edition. In Chapter III, Dickens had written (in

Esther's person) about the fault she had been born with, and of which, she added parenthetically, "I confusedly felt guilty and yet innocent"; this went through three sets of proofs, monthly instalments, and the first edition in book-form unharmed. But in the next edition, that is, the Cheap Edition, "confusedly" was replaced by "confessedly" and the sense of the phrase was ruined, for one can hardly be confessedly innocent! And that change, like all changes for the worse, it would seem, had come to stay, through Library and Charles Dickens Editions and indeed all later editions until this year, including all the respectable ones, Riverside, New Oxford Illustrated, Penguin, and Rinehart, with the exception of the Crowell Press version, which is based on the 1853 text. At the end of Chapter VIII, when Esther and Ada return to Jenny's house after her baby's death, on a mission of mercy, pointedly contrasting with the Pardiggle blatancy, they see Jenny's kind friend. Dickens had written "As she gave way for us, we went softly in, and put what we had brought, near the miserable bed." Thus in proofs, thus again in first edition; but from the Cheap Edition on, *we* is replaced by *she* and the whole sentence becomes what I regard as absolute and unmitigated nonsense: "As she gave way for us, she went softly in, and put what we had brought, near the bed." It is amazing that no editor (with the exception once more of Duane DeVries, who used the correct 1853 text) troubled his head about this, or wondered how a woman could at the same time give way and go in first. Another intriguing reflection is that such absurdities, inadvertently created, never seem to be set right by a later, similar, and symmetrical accident. I am not much given to pessimism in general, but my experience of textual history is that the worst version has most staying power.

With the peculiarities of Dickens' manuscript spelling and punctuation I need not detain you. But perhaps I could add to this sampling of the teachings of textual annotation

examples of what can be found out concerning Dickens'
principles and intentions in proofreading. For instance, a
number of corrections are made with a view to toning down
the resemblance between Harold Skimpole and Leigh Hunt.
Much has been written already on this painful incident, but
the whole truth does not appear to be known yet. Dickens'
letters to Forster show him penitently erasing words and
phrases that would make the identification too obvious, or
asking Forster to do it for him; yet he left a number of
signposts like the speech on bees which is very similar to
something Hunt had written in 1848;[2] it seems that the
whole Skimpole case will have to be re-examined one day by
scholars intimately familiar with the work, life, and conver-
sation of Leigh Hunt; they alone will be able to determine
how far the alterations and cancellations diminished the
resemblance; this is a wild guess of mine, but I should not
be surprised to hear that the resemblance was increased at
some points. Meanwhile, textual notes provide all the
materials for such a quest in convenient form. That the task
is a hard one I should like to illustrate by referring to Skimpole's daughters' names. Mr Skimpole has three daughters
and, in Chapter XLIII, introduces them respectively as "my
Beauty daughter, Arethusa," "my Sentiment daughter,
Laura," and "my Comedy daughter, Kitty." In manuscript,
and until a missing second or third set of proofs, they were
introduced respectively as "my Beauty daughter, Juliet —
a remembrance of Shakespeare," "my Sentiment daughter,
Laura — a remembrance of Petrarch," and "my Comedy
daughter, Susannah — a remembrance of Beaumarchais."
The inference can only be that Juliet and Susannah were too
close to the names of Leigh Hunt's own daughters, while
Laura, Arethusa, and Kitty were not, and that an explicit
literary connection with the names of his offspring would
also have been too readily identifiable. But these assumptions
are not easy to verify. Leigh Hunt himself was strangely — or

naturally — reticent and perhaps ill-informed about the names and number of his own children. In his *Autobiography* he mentions that when he went to Italy in 1821, "my family was numerous," which is true as far as it goes but does not go very far. *The Dictionary of National Biography* is more specific, but probably wrong, in asserting that in 1821 the Hunts had seven children. The prize for accuracy ought to be given probably to a Frenchman, my former master and colleague Louis Landré, whose monumental study of Leigh Hunt[3] mentions Thornton as having been born in 1810 and John in 1812, followed by Mary in 1814. Even Landré nods occasionally, for his next venture in that direction is to the effect that "deux nouveaux enfants" (two new children) had been born in 1818 and 1819; apparently this does *not* mean two children of a new kind or sex; for, by 1821, when the Hunts leave for Italy, Landré counts his, or their, chickens and finds six, that is, neither the five he himself had gradually listed not the seven of *D.N.B.* fame; after all, there was much wisdom in the father's vagueness, "my family was numerous"; five of Landré's six are boys, and in a footnote he forges ahead to the end of this progenitive career, just altering the placing of John, now relegated to third position after Mary; the 1821 contingent thus becomes: Thornton, Mary, John, Swinburne, Percy, and Sylvan. Landré then informs us that Vincent was born in Italy and that two daughters were added later to "the infantine group," named Jacintha and Julia. So that it took all Hunt's pertinacity to achieve what Skimpole had obtained with apparent ease and unconcern: a trio or bouquet of three daughters. One can understand why Juliet had to be dismissed; she was too close to Julia; but was Susannah too much like Jacintha? On the other hand, again, Hunt's *Autobiography* makes no mention of his children by name, with the exception of Vincent, who died very young (and Hunt adds that it is only the second time he ventures to write down his name) and of Mary Florimel, now explaining that Mary was her mother's name (which is not strictly speaking accurate, since Hunt's wife was called Marian) and that Florimel was the name of one of Spenser's heroines. Here may well lie the ultimate reason for the change and especially for leaving out the literary references. Not that Dickens could have read the posthumously published autobiography in 1852, but perhaps Hunt was in the habit of explaining at least that one daughter's name in such terms to his visitors.

Not much of this will be found in the Norton Critical Edition of *Bleak House,* though some of it will find its way into the French Pléiade *Froid Logis.* The principle of the Norton Critical Editions is that readers like to be stimulated by hints and documents to carry out their own investigations. Such is our implied reader. There is a wide field to be explored.

I hope it is clear by now that textual editing in itself implies a great many assumptions about one's readers. The editor's assumptions become more and more articulate as he ventures beyond the text into criticism, biography, and explanatory annotation. Clarendon, Norton and Pléiade policies differ sharply in those respects. Working for the French-speaking readers of the Pléiade contributed in opening my eyes to the existence of the editor's implied reader, because when you are doing two editions of the same novel, you have to become conscious that a whole set of assumptions about your readers changes drastically from one to the other: assumptions, for instance, as to what each class of readers will know or be ignorant of, etc. Translation is itself a form of bridging over the gap between two worlds. The clearest such case would be provided by the characters' names, which are significant in English and obscure as well as rebarbative in French. What will French readers make of Jarndyce or Dedlock? Here it would seem that annotation is indispensable, for no one would wish to perpetrate a sacrilegious alteration of these memorable names and thereby make them unrecognizable to English eyes. Perhaps the Buffy-Cuffy-Duffy and Boodle-Coodle-Doodle sequences are different, for they must be extraordinarily flat to a reader who does not anticipate the crowning effect of Noodle or Puffy. Other difficulties for the translator, as one who establishes communication between author and reader, will be, for instance, the near impossibility of rendering the idiolects of some characters, like Jo, or Bagnet, or Bucket, in *Bleak House;* the greatest impossibility of all, however, is clearly provided by the speech of my distinguished and murderous fellow-countryperson, Ms or Mademoiselle Hortense. There is also a great deal of punning, or wordplay, to torment the translator ruthlessly. The task is a hopeless one.

Not so, or not to the same extent, annotation. Provided that we know for whom we are annotating. Experience shows that the task is endless and often thankless. Hours can be spent on the elucidation of one apparently minor detail; hours can be wasted running after red herrings; frustration lies in store; sometimes one discovers that there was no solution because there was no problem; more often there is no solution although there is a very real problem. And in that case, what is the best policy? Shall we leave the difficulty unannotated, which is in fact tantamount to asserting that it isn't there, that it doesn't exist? That would be Mr Podsnap's policy, no doubt. Shall we have instead one of those empty notes which may be irritating when they are too numerous, I mean the notes that read simply, "Unidentified"; it is easy enough to be sarcastic about such notes, which do not provide much information (although they may have demanded more efforts than some brilliant elucidations achieved by luck, hunch, or fluke). But surely they must be preserved as an appeal for help; the editor assumes readers to be people who read sympathetically, who are members of the vast international brotherhood of scholarly researchers. "Unidentified" (meaning "by me, by us, as yet") may be read as an invitation. Let me give one example of such an appeal which I blame myself for not having made before and which I am therefore making now (after consulting a number of learned people privately and vainly); in Chapter XXXIX of *Bleak House,* there is a reference to Richard Carstone walking thoughtfully in Chancery Lane like many other loungers with "the like bent head, the bitten nail, the lowering eye, the lingering step, the purposeless and dreamy air, the good consuming and consumed, the life turned sour." I have to confess that I fail to understand the words "the good consuming and consumed"; to me they do not have the natural Dickens ring; they sound like a quotation or reference; a note would seem to me to be the proper place for enlisting help in order to solve this problem.

The annotator's constant tools will be the English Bible, as is to be expected, but also the Anglican Book of Common Prayer; Shakespeare, but also Thomas Moore's *Irish Melodies* and a good collection of nursery rhymes; dictionaries of literary quotations and allusions, companions to literature, but also encyclopaedias providing information about sub-literature; maps and atlases and other works about London topography and its history; treatises about various British institutions, especially, of course, the legal system, and the Victorian way of life generally. Annotating one novel involves one in endless research and in reams of correspondence (to use the Copperfieldian phrase about Mr Micawber); the annotator becomes a terrible bore and a plague to his friends, as the man with some two hundred "idées fixes". I suppose it is everybody's experience in the academic world to receive letters of enquiry from annotators. And here the element of luck comes into play. Last year, I had such a letter from a colleague who was editing and annotating one of Balzac's novels, and she stumbled over an allusion to "M. Canning"; you know how these things go; the colleague wrote "if you don't know the answer off-hand, don't bother to etc. etc."; of course I didn't know the answer off-hand; I never do; and of course I bothered; I went to the University Library, I borrowed and read three books on Canning; I did not find the answer to my colleague's query — but I found a great deal of valuable information for two or three notes on *Bleak House*. Last year also, I went to a huge open-air market on a disused airfield in Hertfordshire (*Bleak House* country par excellence); there was one small stand where a man was selling a lot of junk and a few old books; one of these was a *Punch* almanack for the year 1847; I bought it for the sake of the binding and a few good cartoons; but I found it packed with first-rate annotatory material of a kind that is not easy to come by: the exact amount of the tax on hair-powder, the legal cab-fares in London according to distance, the names of all the high officials in the administration.

Some annotations will perhaps be suggested by textual history, as in the case of Skimpole's daughters, which would seem likely to interest all classes of readers. But other notes will be of interest only to specific classes and will thus demand from the editor at least an implicit notion of the reply to the fundamental query "editing for whom?"

As far as *Bleak House* is concerned, I find that both French and American readers must be told something about, for instance, the history of lighting the streets and houses by means of gas, about the exact shape, size, and purpose of the area in a Victorian house (that would be unnecessary in an edition for British readers); Mr Jobling's speech "Ill fo manger, and mangering is as necessary to me as it is to a Frenchman" (in Chapter XX, "pronouncing that word [manger] as if he meant a necessary fixture in an English stable") demands annotation, but differing in kind and extent, for all classes of readers; and that, incidentally, makes one wonder at the linguistic level achieved by Dickens' own implied reader, who got his monthly part for his monthly shilling, and not one word of annotation! Notes presumably required by American readers but not by their French counterparts include: "periods" (Mr Kenge's rounded sentences), "press" in the sense of wardrobe or cupboard (needless to say, these do not demand annotation when they are translated, because the translator has no reason for choosing obsolete or obscure equivalents); the Tuileries (in Paris); Jo's slang (again French equivalents will have to be found and they will not need to be as opaque as "fen larks," "stow hooking it," etc.); "dust-binn," "sweeps," "the whole boiling." Of course the reverse kind of situation is much more frequent, for the barrier of a common language is less high than the wall of a different one; many are the phrases that American readers will presumably take in their stride while French readers will pant for annotation.

The result of these varying needs and demands is that we can find a considerable amount of divergence between editions.

I would like to add a handful of examples from the *Christmas Stories* which will eke out my Pléiade volume. I have found it indispensable to annotate the title of "Tom Tiddler's Ground," to identify the Latin text-book that gave the rules of grammar in Latin (in "the Schoolboy's Story"), to say a word about the Great Bed of Ware ("Holly-Tree Inn"), to comment on the not very esoteric allusion contained in "national-participled" ("Somebody's Luggage") or on the very esoteric name "Parliamentary trains" (in "Mugby Junction," of course); there are a few significant names like Cheeseman, Miss Griffin, Mr Mopes; there are one or two puns, like "dollarous/dolorous" and "the Bard of A-1."

My final example of a possible point for annotation I take from what was long my favourite Christmas Story by Dickens, "Mrs. Lirriper's Lodgings." That worthy and garrulous lady explains that her lodgings in Norfolk Street have no smell of coal-sacks; whoever alludes to a smell of coal-sacks, she says, must be "referring to Arundel or Surrey or Howard but not Norfolk." The names of the four streets are probably unfamiliar to most twentieth-century readers unless they happen to live in that part of London, near the Thames. But one look at a street-map shows what the joke is: Arundel Street and Surrey Street run parallel to Norfolk Street, one on each side, and Howard Street links Surrey to Arundel, cutting across Norfolk; besides, all four are exceedingly close together and form a very tiny corner of London; so that Mrs Lirriper's words are a clear example of her complete bad faith; it would be a miracle if Norfolk Street, surrounded and cut across by coal-smelling streets, were preserved from the same smell. Without a note, the joke will be lost; but if perception of the joke demands a note, the joke will be stale.

On the whole, however, I think the note should be supplied, like every other help to understanding and appreciation (though to enjoyment there are no helps). The claims of a good text no longer need to be militantly asserted, though textual variants may still be unpopular, especially with people who think history (literary history) is bunk; I have met such people and they told me that what the writer actually wrote did not matter; and I have met other people who told me that there is nothing we may properly call the text, and others again (or rather the same, three years later) who told me there is no person we may legitimately call the author; these people are very earnest, and clever, and young, and often sincere in their investigations. But life is short and some of us are getting too old for these intellectually exciting ventures. Meanwhile, among more traditional circles, to which a humdrum editor will assume that his implied readers belong, it is still possible to do much useful work. An editor does not expect much gratitude, or huge earnings; the editor's work is almost concealed, subterranean, or at least unspectacular; the steps are never giant strides for mankind, but they are more definitely a progress, however infinitesimal, than the results achieved through most of the other tasks a literary scholar is called upon to accomplish.

NOTES

1 See G.A. Bonnard, ed., *English Studies Today.* Second Series, Bern, Francke Verlag, 1961, pp. 187-95. This article originated in a paper read at a conference held in Lausanne in August 1959.

2 In *A Jar of Honey from Mount Hybla* (1848); see Chapter XI.

3 See *Leigh Hunt (1784-1859). Contribution à l'histoire du Romantisme anglais. I. L'auteur (d'après des documents nouveaux),* Paris, Belles-Lettres, 1935.

# Textual Problems
# in Editing Thackeray

# Peter Shillingsburg

Forty-five years or so ago my father, at that time a ministerial student in a small school in Minneapolis, delivered a student sermon in hermeneutics class on the great commission: Go ye into all the world and preach the gospel. Just as he was warming to the subject and reaching his most telling points, the bell rang and his audience scattered to other classes, leaving only one convert down front — himself, who spent the next forty years as a missionary. I hope the bell does not ring before I finish, but it does seem to me that the main audience for my remarks today is myself. That is, in preparing this paper I have learned what are to me new things about what a textual editor is, the nature of his job as an editor, and the nature of what he produces. For many of you, I fear, I may be saying things about editing that you already know quite well, but perhaps the circumstances of the publication histories of Thackeray's works which I mention on the way will keep you from wishing too much for the saving bell.

Though the details concerning the composition and printing of Thackeray's works and the editorial problems they present are unique, the overall patterns are familiar to textual editors. The output is formidable enough: six major novels, ten minor ones, six Christmas books, three travel books, three collections of essays, a collection of ballads, sixteen collections of stories and short novels, ten or so ephemeral separate publications, and some two to three hundred additional magazine items collected, if at all, only posthumously. Most of the novels appeared in three or four separate editions in Thackeray's lifetime; and, so far as I have determined, at least one of the reprints of each work usually shows signs of authorial revision.

Manuscript attrition is, unfortunately, more extensive for Thackeray than for some other major Victorian novelists. Manuscripts and proofs exist sporadically for the middle works with slightly more for the later works, but there was no Forster to collect and save Thackeray's manuscripts — and these, instead, sometimes went in bits and pieces to his former friends and admirers as mementos after his death. The manuscripts for *Henry Esmond, The Rose and the Ring, The Wolves and the Lamb, The Adventures of Philip, The Four Georges, Lovel the Widower,* and *The Roundabout Papers* are nearly complete; substantial portions of *The Newcomes* and *The Virginians* are still extant. But besides the almost total absence of other manuscripts and only rare instances of surviving proofs, the student of Thackeray's manuscripts is vexed by the lack of any centre in which to study them. London and New York contain important collections, but so do Cambridge (Trinity College), Harvard, Princeton, Yale, the University of Texas, the Huntington Library, and Charterhouse School (no longer in London). At least eight other institutions not in New York or London own portions of Thackeray manuscript other than letters; and book auction records suggest that a number of individuals also own at least fragments.[1]

Multiple editions and lost manuscripts are not the only problems an editor of Thackeray shares with the editors of other major Victorians. Multiple printings within an edition provided ample opportunity for variation, and when the book is a parts-issued book, the complications are next to incredible. In the production and publication of a Victorian novel in parts there were several different processes going on simultaneously or at least overlapping in time, each of which left its distinctive mark on sections of the book. The *printing* process began before publication but continued after it in the form of unannounced, identically dated, reprints; *publication* began with the first issue of the first part, but the term also applies to the first issue of the first volume (a year or more after publication of the parts began) and to the first issue of the second volume, if there was one (another year later); *binding* was almost an individual matter with each book at each stage of issue and involves certain contemporary as well as modern *re*-bindings. The combination of these processes could and did produce editions of almost infinite intra-edition variation. The first issue of the first printing of each part is, perhaps, not so difficult to determine, but, after that, printings are difficult to identify and the mixtures of sheets from different printings complicate things radically. Since the number of copies specified in the initial print-order for each part often varied, one or more parts of a volume could be (and were) reprinted before the first issue in book form. Usually second and subsequent printings were executed *before* previously printed stock was exhausted. If new-printed sheets were stacked on top of first-printed sheets in the bindery, and if binding proceeded from the top of the stack, then, in the case of sheets reprinted before book-form issue, earlier issued parts could contain sheets printed later than those in the later issued books. When this activity is carried on for fifteen years, as it was for *Vanity Fair* and *Pendennis*, with small reprint orders called for by part number (i.e., only parts of the book reprinted from time to time, not the whole book reprinted together) and even smaller binding orders placed as the need arose, and when all this is compounded by continuous issue of the edition both in parts and book form and by purchasers separately ordering bindings for the parts they purchased one at a time — when all these conditions exist, as they did for all Thackeray's parts-issued books except *The Virginians,* then an identifying description of one or even five copies will leave hundreds of other copies undescribed. I have collated five copies of the first edition of *Vanity Fair* and located over two hundred and thirty variants ranging from altered punctuation to omitted illustrations, and from word changes to the fortuitously accurate resetting of type for whole pages, and, of course, a great deal of type-damage besides. Nevertheless I have not found copies representing all the variants that David Randall reported in his "Notes Toward a Correct Collation of the First Edition of *Vanity Fair.*"[2]

It is perhaps obligatory in a discussion of editorial problems to mention authorial intentions, since, willy-nilly, every editor has to face the question of what his author wanted. I do not care to get much entangled in the philosophical intricacies of the problem of intention, but I do recognize that they are there.[3] I find the distinction between a *work* and a *text* to be useful in considering the problem of Thackeray's intentions and in dealing with the evidence that survives as a guide to what he wanted. A *text,* according to Professor Todd Bender,[4] is a rigid document representing one version of a work as it exists in a given manuscript or printed source. A *work,* on the other hand, is the fluid, developing, and changing piece of writing which is represented, more or less well, in the various texts which survive. It is important from this distinction, in the case of Thackeray, to realize that a work can have not only several stages of development but more than one stage of intended completion, and that an editor must use his judgment in choosing which intention he wants his text to represent. First intentions may seem more desirable than last intentions, or artistic intentions more than those which were motivated by economic considerations. The Thackeray edition I am preparing seeks to present first intentions; that is, it will try to present the text as it would have been had ideal conditions prevailed at the time of first publication. There are several reasons for choosing first, rather than revised, intentions. In a book such as *Pendennis*, for example, the revised version of 1856 seems in my judgment to be reduced in stature. It is about eighteen printed pages and 179 illustrations shorter than the original publication; only two additions are made and these merely smooth elisions; 758 substantial changes were made (including 203 major omissions or word substitutions, 180 corrections of errors in the first edition, and 375 other alterations of some consequence but of the kind normally undertaken by printers and editors). In addition, over 1200 inconsequential changes in accidentals were made. There is no extant external evidence that Thackeray made any of the changes himself. But though I once argued that the revisions may have been carried out by an amanuensis, the deftness of some of them makes it seem more likely that Thackeray made the major revisions himself. The nature of the changes, however, and their total effect are more important in my decision to present first intentions than are the magnitude of individual changes or their authority. Whether or not Thackeray made the changes and whether or not the revision was a careful one (I think, by the way, that it was not), the changes seem to be largely the acquiescent response to public criticism of *Vanity Fair* and *Pendennis*. After all, seven years had elapsed and the reviser of *Pendennis* was a good bit better off and mellower than its author had been. The total effect of the revision is to dull the biting edges of the book.

My new edition of *Pendennis*, then, will ignore the 1200 or so inconsequential changes introduced in the revised version; it will accept as part of the text the 180 corrections of errors; it will record the 203 major changes in a table so that the revisions that are most likely to have authority can be studied easily; and it will record the 375 other minor but possibly authorial alterations in another table so that my decisions can be examined and, perhaps, disagreed with.

But even for works without the dramatic revisions of *Pendennis,* I am presenting first intentions and arranging the works in my edition in chronological order so that they can be read essentially as Thackeray's first audience read them — as they were first published without the tempering of second thoughts by a mellowing, more comfortable author. They will, thus, reflect more accurately the development and diminishment of Thackeray's work.

There is another distinction with a bearing on authorial intention that I used not to make clearly enough: the one between what the author wrote and what he intended to write. The evidence for what he wrote is impure enough in cases where only the printed forms have survived. Distinguishing between what Thackeray wrote and what some secretary, printer, or publisher's proofreader wrote when the evidence no longer exists is possible only on the basis of the editor's judgment. However, determining what an author intended when an intervening person changed things is only slightly different from determining what was intended when the intervention is that of the author's own fallible fingers or of the author's failure to put in the manuscript all that he expected to see in his proofs.

To sum up what I have been trying to explore: Thackeray, like many authors, left works in more than one completed form, each of which may have a legitimate claim for presentation. And determining, on a word by word basis, what the author wrote or intended to write often requires editorial judgment — it is not necessarily a mechanical process nor is there necessarily one invariably applicable formula for recovering the author's intentions. If methods can vary and if editorial judgment is involved in preparing a scholarly edition, it follows that there can be no such thing as *a* definitive text. Even where only one text is extant, there can be legitimate disagreement over emendations designed to correct the text or restore what the author probably wrote. In short, it is a naive idealism that claims an editor establishes a text for all time. A critical edition presents a version of a work and provides the materials, when they exist, for the study of the development of that work.

The Thackeray edition I am preparing has raised other editorial problems I have not seen much discussed, though again these problems may be common to other editions, especially illustrated ones. Three of Thackeray's major novels and a good many of his minor works were illustrated by the author himself. Though as an artist Thackeray has had from the beginning both admirers and detractors, little was written about the importance of his illustrations to the text until the late 1950s. It is now a critical commonplace that the illustrations add a dimension of their own, commenting ironically and even iconographically on the text.[5] The most obvious instances, probably, are the illustrations of the good Samaritan in vignette initial letters in several books or in pictures hanging on the walls of interior scenes in the larger illustrations. Devils, simpering couples, serpents, mermaids (or sirens rather), churches, and nursing mothers crop up in initial vignettes to comment on the novels' action. In *Vanity Fair* the full page illustration titled "Becky's second appearance in the character of Clytemnestra" shows Jos in his room in the Elephant Hotel pleading with Dobbin for help. On the wall is a picture of the good Samaritan, and behind the curtain stands Becky with an evil look and what might pass for a vial of poison in her hand. The text does not say that Becky overheard Jos's plea nor that she killed the cowardly fat man, but the illustration leaves little that actually needs to be written out on that score. At the same time the picture on the wall raises tantalizingly ambiguous questions as to which of the three is the victim by the wayside, which is the good Samaritan, and which the Pharisee passing by on the other side.

Editorially, the question is not whether to include the illustrations, but what to use for copy-text. Thackeray experimented from time to time, especially in the 1830s and 40s, with transferring his drawings onto woodcuts and engraved plates himself, but he was not good at it and for the most part relied on others to transfer his drawings to a printing medium. Occasionally he drew directly on a wood-block, but even then the woodcut itself was the work of another more or less skilled hand.[6]

In the 1850s and 60s Thackeray came more and more to prefer one engraver's shop — that of Swain — and insisted that as much as possible of the work should be done there, but he was still bedevilled by workmanship which did not satisfy him but had to be used anyway for lack of time or money to replace it. In fact, Thackeray occasionally invited problems of this sort by writing instructions to the craftsmen on how to change his drawing: leave out the extra figure from the front seat of the coach, he instructed the engraver of an illustration for *The Yellowplush Correspondence* in 1839. And for the vignette of the author grasping Time by the forelock in Chapter 2 of *Lovel the Widower* (1860), the drawing is accompanied by both an instruction for change and a mild warning to follow copy: "Make the oval regular [it was slightly tilted and sketchy in the drawing] & Time stepping out of the O" (just as it is in the drawing). In short, Thackeray provided copy which was both improved according to instructions and botched according to the ability of the artisan.

An editor is left at times with a choice between an unfinished drawing and a somewhat distorted woodcut or plate. The ideal would be to print one in the text and the other as a variant at the back, or, perhaps, to give Thackeray's original drawing to a new engraver for transferral to a printing medium. The expense and small likelihood of successful results probably preclude the latter, but choice of copy-text for Thackeray's illustrations is not yet a settled issue.

Another editorial problem raised by the Thackeray edition involves distinguishing the author and the narrator. Thackeray wrote under a large number of pseudonyms, creating in many cases a narrative persona of sharply defined characteristics. When such a pseudonymous character is practically illiterate and writes in the first person, as Charles Edward Harrington Fitzroy Yellowplush did, special editorial problems arise. "The Yellowplush Correspondence" was published in *Fraser's Magazine* in 1837-38 and 1840. No manuscript survives. Seven separate editions were printed in Thackeray's lifetime. It was pirated by Carey and Hart of Philadelphia in 1837 in an edition with no authority. Thackeray had something (just what is not clear) to do with the republication in *Comic Tales and Sketches* (London, 1841). Baudry in Paris used the *Comic Tales* text for a reprint in the same year. Eleven years later Appleton of New York included it in their pirated reprint of a series of Thackeray's works. Four years later, in 1856, Thackeray used his own copies of the unauthorized Appleton text to prepare the London *Miscellanies* which in turn were used as copy for the 1856 Tauchnitz edition in Leipzig. Now, although Thackeray was involved in preparing the 1841 *Comic Tales* and the 1856 *Miscellanies,* it is not clear which of the changes are his and which are the printer's. *Comic Tales* introduced over 700 new readings of which over 290 are spelling changes. Yellowplush writes in a pseudo-cockney dialect — though he somehow renders the speech of educated persons in standard English. Almost any spelling change can be authorial since misspellings are as common as correct spellings. In the first edition Yellowplush's spelling is more varied than in subsequent editions because more correct spellings or "standard" Yellowplushian spellings are introduced than are new possibly Yellowplushian spellings. In any event, the lack of external evidence makes it difficult to say whether a word is misspelled by intention or accident.

A look at some statistics, however, helps to give an idea of the authority — or lack of it — of the spelling changes. *Comic Tales* introduced close to 720 changes, for all of which the authority is in question. Appleton, based on *Comic Tales,* introduced 523 additional changes of which twenty-nine fortuitously restored original readings. The Appleton changes are all without authority. The 1856 *Miscellanies,* based on the Appleton text, introduced 628 new readings, of which sixty-six restored original readings changed by Appleton, and thirty restored original readings first changed by *Comic Tales.* The overall result was that by 1856 the "authorized" text in the *Miscellanies* differed from the original printing in about 1733 readings.

In the absence of evidence which would show who made the changes, one must either choose a text and reproduce it as is or else rely on editorial judgment. Which changes seem likely to be Thackeray's? In my opinion, only sixty-eight of the changes represent corrections Thackeray either made, or approved, or would have approved. They include changing *friend* to *feind* in the expression "the foul fiend" (I take the misspelling of *fiend* to be intentional on Thackeray's part but inadvertent on Yellowplush's), the change from *twelve* to *eleven* as the number of Mr Shum's daughters who trooped in to witness Mary Shum's disgrace, and the change of *ensered* to *entered* (*ensered* not seeming to me a possible cockney or Yellowplushian spelling for *entered*).

The principle I have followed is to try to learn the range of possibilities and spelling habits of Yellowplush, purging what can be shown to be outright errors and curbing what seems incompatible with Yellowplush's erratic system. It was tempting, I admit, to think that *antelope* was an erroneous spelling for *envelope*, especially when a subsequent edition changed it to *anvelope*, or that *smears* was an inappropriate cockney rendering of *sneers*, or that *miserandum* was an error for *mimerandum* used in later editions — but Yellowplush has a propensity for punning malapropisms which make these readings possible though not phonetically accurate.

This kind of editorial problem and the procedures I have followed entail two responsibilities: recording the changes I have made in an attempt to correct the text, and recording the changes made by the other authorial editions. It is not very likely that everyone will agree with my decisions, but users of my edition will be able to see the alternatives and judge for themselves. Spelling is not the only difficulty, but I have dwelt on it as an illustration of the special problems posed by an author writing in the persona of an illiterate, but doing so in such a way that a certain importance attaches to the manner in which the author shows the illiteracy. My analysis of the variants leads me to believe that compositors or publisher's editors had a good deal of private fun making Yellowplush conform to their own image of his special brand of illiteracy.

Of the remaining 1665 new readings, forty-nine seem to me of sufficient importance and appropriateness to make it credible that Thackeray might have made them. These include spelling changes, the addition or deletion of words, and some punctuation changes. The rest are of such neutral or negative effect that hard evidence alone would make me believe Thackeray made or approved them. This conclusion is reached not just by applying the principle that punctuation, capitalization, and other matters of form are generally the province of editors; it is based to some extent on an extra-polation from surviving manuscripts and proofs for other Thackeray works. Not a great deal of this material survives, and one cannot assume a similarity between extant materials and lost materials of ten years earlier, but there is really little else with which to guide one's judgment.

There are two aspects of the extant manuscripts and proofs which attract attention. One is the extent and nature of Thackeray's involvement in proof correction, and the other is the degree to which the manuscripts are a full and fair indication of Thackeray's intentions. Legend has it that Thackeray read proof only sporadically and then carelessly. This is a tradition based on Thackeray's off-handed statements about his writing, on Anthony Trollope's accusations of his lack of diligence, and on a cursory examination by a succession of Thackeray students of portions of the scanty and much-scattered manuscript and proof materials. The first steps toward correcting that view have been taken by Edgar Harden in a series of articles on the making of the serialized novels. Professor Harden is the first person to seek out and examine in detail the full range of extant pre-publication forms of Thackeray's work. He has collected and substantially augmented his published articles for a book forthcoming from the University of Georgia Press. I am indebted to him and the Georgia Press for a preview of the book, for my ideas and conclusions about the nature of Thackeray's manuscripts have been influenced by the material he has gathered. Upsetting the popular conception, Professor Harden shows that the serial novels went through more than one set of proofs. It is true that Thackeray would often be writing a serial part in the very month it was due at the printer, but it is not true that he rattled off a manuscript for the printer's devil waiting at the door, who then raced to the printshop where the manuscript became a book without further ado on the author's part. A typical procedure was for Thackeray to send a half to two-thirds of a serial part to the printer while he continued working. He would get first proofs, figure how much more was required for the number, and add material accordingly. The corrected first part with the addition then went to the printer and new proofs were sent to Thackeray. As I have said, there are not many proofs extant, and they show that many of the proof alterations were substantial revisions and additions of the sort one would expect in the process of adjusting length. It is worth noting, however, that not only are there single-word changes, but on occasion there are large cuts, even in numbers where the cutting entailed the writing of extra material to supply the required length. Those of you familiar with the traditional view of Thackeray as proofreader probably doubt this model. However, for one number of *The Virginians* there are extant at the Pierpont Morgan Library portions of the manuscript, marked first proofs, marked second proofs, and the published version, which contains further changes not marked in the second proofs — indicating another no longer extant proof stage. The absence of similar material for other numbers is not evidence that similar proofing schedules were not followed. Several other parts of *The Virginians* and of *Pendennis* and *The Newcomes* show evidence of more than one proof stage. Another point I wish to emphasize is that Thackeray also occasionally changed punctuation in the extant proofs.

Having established that Thackeray did, at least some of the time, read and correct proofs, and that he occasionally, though not often, altered punctuation in proof, we can turn to the manuscripts with the question: to what extent do they represent what Thackeray wanted (or intended) to see in print?

The nature of a Thackeray manuscript can be illustrated by the first two chapters of the manuscript for *Vanity Fair* — the equivalent of about fifteen printed pages. It contains numerous ampersands and the abbreviations of *which* and *would,* all of which the printers of course expanded. Although there is a good deal of dialogue, Thackeray did not use double quotes and his single quotes usually indicate only the opening or ending of a speech. Furthermore, a dash is used quite as often as quotation marks to show speech and quite often, again, there is no indication beyond context. At least twenty-five times in these fifteen pages the printers supplied quotation marks where Thackeray had none, and I believe they missed three others. Initial expletives like *Well* or *Now* seldom are followed by a comma, nor is that mark always used to separate words in a series: in the manuscript commas are omitted from the description of Miss Pinkerton's farewell to Amelia as "dull pompous and tedious"; and a few lines earlier there are no commas in the mythical Jones's description of the novel as "excessively foolish trivial twaddling and ultra-sentimental." In fact, though Thackeray used commas in the manuscript, the printed version contains, according to a quick count, 347 additional commas, while omitting four which Thackeray had supplied. About thirty-seven manuscript dashes were changed to other marks of punctuation: semicolons, colons, commas, periods or double quotation marks. About twenty manuscript colons became semicolons, while two manuscript semicolons became colons; twenty-six hyphens were added where the manuscript had two separate words; and seventeen lowercase letters were capitalized. There were about twenty other additions: six apostrophes, three colons, three semicolons, one question mark, four exclamation points, three italicizations – all added where the manuscript had nothing, and these marks were interchanged in about sixty other instances. There are four cases of a manuscript word ending in *or* or *ize* being changed to *our* or *ise* and *dixonary* becomes *dictionary.* The total number of changes between the manuscript and the first edition in the first fifteen printed pages is over 600. Of these only twenty are word changes.

It seems a fair conclusion to draw that the manuscript is inadequately punctuated and that Thackeray intended the printers to supply conventional punctuation. That was the practice of the time and Thackeray was enough of a journalist and newspaperman to know what he could expect from the printers. However, having left much of the punctuating to the printers, he reviewed it. We know from surviving proofs for *The Newcomes, The Virginians,* and some of the works first published in the *Cornhill Magazine* that he occasionally called for changes in the printer's punctuation. Since he read proof — often in more than one stage — he can even be said to have tacitly approved the punctation of the first printed version. We can assume for the most part, I think, that if Thackeray disapproved of any of the printer's punctuation, it probably did not survive in the first edition. Exceptions might be identified by comparing the manuscript with the printed form, but the introduction of punctuation judged to be inferior or even erroneous is not proof positive that Thackeray's intentions were violated.

But at least two problems remain. Why did Thackeray rely so heavily on the printers, and does it follow that the punctuation of the first edition is, somehow, Thackeray's since he seems to have "approved" it?

I do not have an answer to the first problem. Either Thackeray trusted the printers to do an adequate job which he would have the opportunity to check at proof stage — he had had, after all, a greal deal of experience in the ten years preceding *Vanity Fair* and, as I said before, would know what to expect; or, on the other hand, he may have known that printers would impose their own system of punctuation regardless of what he did, and either from despair or lack of interest he concluded that the difference between his and their pointing systems was not worth the constant battle it would take to have his own way.

The second problem is less difficult. I think it cannot be

said that the first edition punctuation represents what Thackeray intended. I would argue, in fact, that there is *no* guide to what Thackeray intended. The manuscript is inadequate in this regard; it was clearly expected that printers would augment the manuscript punctuation. The manuscript cannot even be said to indicate Thackeray's preference for light punctuation. There is too much missing; he had to have intended more punctuation than he supplied in the manuscript, but there is no way of knowing just how far those intentions went. His reliance on the printers and his apparent approval of what they did is evidence only of what Thackeray tolerated.

One of the implications of this conclusion is that any stylistic analysis of Thackeray's writing which relies on punctuation can say little about Thackeray. It must be based either on the printer-supplied punctuation which everyone read, or on the manuscript punctuation which Thackeray did not intend to be considered finished. The editor has two choices: he can start with the manuscript and try to do for Thackeray what Thackeray wanted his printer to do for him, or he can accept the punctuation of the first edition, checking it against the manuscript for instances of perceptible distortion which may have escaped Thackeray's proofreading eye. In either case, the editor cannot hope to say that his edition *recovers* Thackeray's intentions, but only that he has tried to fulfil those intentions as his judgment and imagination have led him to understand them.

Practically speaking, either approach followed by a single editor should result in virtually the same text — that is, the editor choosing the manuscript as copy-text would probably supply about the same punctuation as was supplied by the original printer, since all indications are that Thackeray intended conventional pointing to be imposed; and what could be a better guide to that than a contemporary publishing house. On the other hand, the editor starting with

the first edition would probably restore only those manuscript readings that he thought were distorted by the printer's
punctuation. It could, of course, be argued that Thackeray's
writing habits in letters and works such as *The Rose and the
Ring* which were intended for readers other than printers
would be a better guide to his intentions for his published
works, but that is argument by analogy which cannot be
conclusive and, besides, would be extremely difficult in
practice.[7]

Against the background of a decade or more of "definitive"
editions and "established texts," the conclusion that Thackeray's intentions concerning punctuation are irrecoverable
may seem wishy-washy or disappointing; but it seems to
me simply honest to assert only what the extant evidence
allows and to admit that a critical edition is perhaps no better
than the critical judgment behind editorial decisions.

The reconsideration of these questions has brought home
to me more than ever that the nature of the actual textual
problems he encounters determines the course an editor
follows quite as much as any set of preconceived principles
or rules of editing. One constantly hears objections to
editors who, oblivious to the scholarship on editing, guide
themselves by the seat of their pants. A good deal can be
said on behalf of principle and method in order to curb
editorial eccentricities and excesses, but I have chosen to
emphasize the other side because such a great deal has
already been said on the theory of editing correctly and
"definitively." During my tenure as coordinator of the
Center for Scholarly Editions I heard several persons express-
ing interest in a how-to manual on editing. Such a manual
might be helpful in suggesting procedures for beginners so
that, for example, they will do their bibliographical work
before undertaking the editorial, and will clear copyright
permissions before publishing; nevertheless, I cannot see that
matters have altered since A. E. Housman wrote that you can

have hard and fast rules if you want them but they will be false rules and lead you wrong and that when it comes to editing "Knowledge is good, method is good, but one thing beyond all others is necessary, and that is to have a head, not a pumpkin, on your shoulders, and brains, not pudding, in your head."[8]

## NOTES

1  A preliminary census of library locations for Thackeray's manuscripts is printed in *Costerus,* 2 (1974), 333-59, and supplemented from time to time in the *Thackeray Newsletter.*

2  *Papers of the Bibliographical Society of America,* 42 (1948), 95-109.

3  For a survey and commentary on discussions of the philosophical problem, see G. Thomas Tanselle, "The Editorial Problem of Final Intention," *Studies in Bibliography,* 29 (1976), 167-211, which expands on aspects of the problem considered in his "Greg's Theory of Copy-Text and the Editing of American Literature," *Studies in Bibliography,* 28 (1975), 167-229.

4  "Literary Texts in Electronic Storage: The Editorial Potential," *Computers in the Humanities,* 10 (1976), 193. One should perhaps add the word *document,* for a manuscript with pen slips or a printed document with misprints may be said to misrepresent a *text* which in turn is only one version of the *work.* Furthermore, a manuscript, typescript, or printed *document* which has been laid aside and then revised can be said to represent two *texts,* both at least partly recoverable.

5  A list of critical commentaries on the relation between text and illustration in Thackeray's work is in Peter L. Shillingsburg, "Thackeray's *Pendennis:* A Rejected Page of Manuscript," *Huntington Library Quarterly,* 38 (1975), 189-95, n. 7. To these can be added Robert F. Kaufman, "The Relationship Between Illustration and Text in the Novels of Dickens, Thackeray, Trollope and Hardy" (Dissertation, New York University, 1974); Robin Sheets, "Art and

Artistry in *Vanity Fair*," *ELH,* 42 (1975), 420-32; Teona Tone Gneiting, "The Pencil's Role in *Vanity Fair*," *Huntington Library Quarterly*, 39 (1976), 171-202; Winslow Rogers, "Art and Artists in *The Newcomes*," *Ball State University Forum* (forthcoming); J. W. Williamson, "Thackeray's Mirror," *Tennessee Studies in Literature* (forthcoming); and Viola H. Winner, "Thackeray and Richard Doyle, the 'Wayward Artist' of *The Newcomes*," *Harvard Library Bulletin* (forthcoming).

6  I am indebted to Mr Nicholas Pickwoad for advice and information on the production and printing of Thackeray's drawings. Mr Pickwoad's Oxford University thesis (near completion) is on Thackeray's published drawings.

7  Perhaps further analysis of the manuscript punctuation will lead to a more satisfactory solution. One possibility that looks attractive is to distinguish between kinds of punctuation, such as sentence-endings and apostrophes which are hopelessly erratic, on the one hand, and internal punctuation which appears generally sufficient as it stands in the manuscript, on the other.

8  A. E. Housman, "The Application of Thought to Textual Criticism," (1921); reprinted in *Selected Prose,* Cambridge: Cambridge University Press, 1961, p. 150.

# The Making and Unmaking of Hardy's Wessex Edition

## Michael Millgate

Perhaps no single quality is more characteristic of Hardy's literary career than his professionalism. Though he became in the course of time a major poet as well as a major novelist, he never lost the feeling that it was, in some sense, his business to supply his readers with what they wanted, and he was unfailingly meticulous in his observation of those contractual obligations to editors and publishers which he had explicitly or implicitly undertaken. Although he was at first innocent of the ways of the literary marketplace, selling outright the copyright of *Under the Greenwood Tree* for thirty pounds — a sum which no inflation factor can convert into respectability — Hardy soon made himself into a thoroughly professional man of letters whose shrewd management did much to keep his books in print and before the public. Realistically if reluctantly he accepted the publishing conventions and conditions as they existed in his time, including the bowdlerizing tendencies of magazine editors and the absence, until almost the end of his novel-writing days, of copyright protection in the United States. He could never quite reconcile himself, however, to the unreliability of printers and always made a point of reading and correcting his own proofs – and often revises of those proofs – with painstaking care and attention to detail. He developed in the process an unusually sharp eye for both the technical and aesthetic aspects of typography and book production and played an active part not only in the preparation of the illustrations for several of his stories as they were serialized in magazines but also in the design of those same works when they first appeared in volume form. Admirable as this professionalism was in many respects, the scholarly editor finds himself confronting special problems precisely as a result of Hardy's concerns – exercised throughout his long life – for, first, the accessibility, second, the accuracy, and third – though by no means a poor third – the physical appearance of his text.

Though it will be for many of you a familiar story, it may be useful to begin by rehearsing the broad outlines of Hardy's career as a publishing novelist – a career similar enough in its details to that of many another Victorian writer but remarkable as a whole for the proliferation of different textual forms over a long period of years. Hardy published his first novel, *Desperate Remedies,* in 1871, when he was thirty-one years old. It appeared first in book form, as did its immediate successor, *Under the Greenwood Tree,* but with his third novel, *A Pair of Blue Eyes,* Hardy fell into that standard Victorian pattern of magazine serialization followed by publication in two or three volumes which was to govern all of his subsequent works of fiction – except that first book publication of his last two novels and of his last three short-story collections was in one-volume form. There were more or less simultaneous American serializations and first editions of almost all these works, also Tauchnitz editions for distribution on the continent of Europe and Colonial Editions for sale in Australia, India, and occasionally Canada — where, however, they seem to have been swamped by the cheaper American editions, both authorized and pirated. In England itself most of the novels appeared in cheap one-volume editions within a few years of their first publication, and in the eighteen-eighties and early eighteen-nineties Sampson Low published several of them in formats sufficiently matching to constitute an *ad hoc* collected edition, though by no means a complete one.

In 1895 Hardy managed to get the rights to all his fiction — apart from *Under the Greenwood Tree* — transferred to Osgood, McIlvaine, a semi-independent English subsidiary of Harper & Brothers of New York, and embarked with them upon the first collected edition proper — called the "Wessex Novels" edition but usually referred to as the Osgood, McIlvaine edition to distinguish it clearly from the later Wessex Edition. Hardy's revisions at this time were extensive — especially though by no means exclusively in matters relating to the topography of his fictional region — and he also wrote for the edition a series of brief but important prefaces. His last two novels first appeared as volumes in the edition — *Jude* in 1895, *The Well-Beloved* in 1897 — and in 1898 Hardy marked his permanent shift to poetry with the publication of *Wessex Poems.* The one volume of prose which was still to follow, *A Changed Man* of 1914, was simply a gathering of stories published long before, so that by the time the first volumes of the Wessex Edition appeared in 1912 Hardy was a man in his early seventies who thought of himself as a poet and had not written a novel for nearly two decades. Indeed, it is worth keeping in mind that while we shall be exclusively concerned this afternoon with the prose volumes of the Wessex Edition, the Edition in its complete form also included six volumes of verse — of which the last, containing *Human Shows* and *Winter Words,* appeared posthumously in 1931. A topographical guide, *Thomas Hardy's Wessex,* written and illustrated by Hermann Lea — with a good deal of co-operation and supervision from Hardy himself — was published in the same format in 1913.

The immediate history of the Wessex Edition — that is to say, the process directed specifically towards the production of the volumes gathered under that general title — began in October 1910 with a proposal from an American publisher for an *édition de luxe* of Hardy's works. Hardy agreed, on the understanding that the texts of all the volumes would be re-set, that he would himself correct the proofs, and that the spelling would not be American.[1] When the arrangements with the American publisher fell through, Hardy's English publisher, Macmillan, substituted the idea of an English "definitive" edition with an initial printing of 1,000 copies instead of the 250 originally planned; the price would be 7s. 6d. per volume, of which Hardy would get 1s. 6d.[2] Hardy adopted the term "definitive" and did much to give it validity. Macmillan supplied him with copies of the "Uniform Edition" which they had had in print since they became his publishers in 1902, and Hardy gave these another thorough revision before submitting them as a printer's copy for the new edition. He took the opportunity to revise and up-date the authorial prefaces, add an entirely new "General Preface," and divide the prose volumes of the edition into categories indicative of his personal valuations of them. This latter innovation, he observed to Sir Frederick Macmillan, was chiefly designed to give journalists something to talk about.[3]

Hardy also supplied Macmillan with his own map of his fictional Wessex, suggesting that it could either be used as it stood or professionally redrawn with the addition of ships, fishes, trees, and other decorative devices such as the old map-makers had affected.[4] Macmillan chose the second of these alternatives and Hardy subsequently gave his warm approval to the proof of the map, with its whale- and dolphin-crowded seas;[5] he did not, however, get his wish for a fold-out map rather than one sewn into the binding with an obscuring crease down the middle. It was Hardy, too, who specified both the photographer (Hermann Lea) and the individual photographs to be used as frontispieces to the successive volumes, and while there is perhaps a hint here of a desire to emulate the photographic frontispieces to Henry James's New York Edition it is worth remembering that Hardy had for many years been in the habit of advising the illustrators of his books and even of providing them with sketches of specific episodes. When the proofs of the Wessex Edition came he read them with the same care as he had given to the planning of the edition, and it was entirely characteristic that he should have pointed out, quite early on, that the new pages, though no wider than those of comparable editions of other authors, were approximately three print-lines longer, and therefore looked unusually tall.[6] The point was indeed well taken, and if Macmillan had acted upon it at the time we might well have had a cheap photographic reprint of the Wessex Edition long before now.

Hardy, then, put much time and trouble into the Wessex Edition and had no hesitation in speaking of it as "definitive" and thinking of it as final: he told Sydney Cockerell in May 1912 that he was going through his books in search of errors "for the last time."[7] The Edition's claim to be considered "the last authority in questions of text," as Richard Purdy puts it in his indispensable bibliography,[8] rests on solid ground, and scholars and critics have every reason to be grateful to Hardy for providing them with so reliable and convenient a point of reference — though they haven't always carried their gratitude so far as actually to use the edition in their work. But if grateful, why not satisfied? What can be added or enhanced by scholarly enterprise and editorial labour? Obviously that isn't a question to which I can under-take a comprehensive answer this afternoon, but I can at least indicate some of the constituent elements of an answer: one or two of them, indeed, are already implicit in the account I have just given.

For all Hardy's devotion to the task of revision and correction there remains the irreducible fact that he was not starting from first principles but working with a text that had itself long lost the bloom and innocence of youth. The volumes of the Macmillan Uniform Edition in which he inscribed his corrections for the Wessex Edition were in fact impressions (some incorporating minor revisions) from the plates of the Osgood, McIlvaine collected edition, which had itself absorbed the plates of the first editions of *Life's Little Ironies* and *A Group of Noble Dames* and the so-called "Fifth Edition" of *Tess of the d'Urbervilles.* The Osgood plates had already been used for a number of Harper printings before Macmillan took them over in 1902, and most of them had been used more than once by Macmillan before Hardy received his copies in 1911 — that of *The Woodlanders,* the only one known to survive, is dated 1906. To inquire into the making of the Wessex Edition, therefore, is necessarily to investigate the making of the Uniform so-called "edition," which is in turn to open up fresh vistas stretching back to the very inception of each work. Hardy's habit of preparing printer's copy for each successive edition by making corrections to the latest printing of the previous edition was natural enough in itself, as well as sensible from an economic point of view, and it has certainly been duplicated by many other authors. But I scarcely need expatiate to an audience such as this upon the textual costs in terms of accumulated errors, the depredations of plate-batter, and so on.

I think it is also possible to argue that it may lead to a certain deadening of responsiveness on the part of the revising author — at least of one as popular and as often reprinted as Hardy — a somewhat wearisome sense of familiarity which is inimical to the closest kind of critical attention. (Henry

James's radical ways with the text of the New York Edition may have had more than a little to do with his very unfamiliarity with the experience of revising for new editions.) Very much to the point here is the question of Hardy's punctuation. Hardy did when revising make changes to the accidentals as well as to the substantives of his text, but it seems to me that such changes are generally in the spirit of a copy-editor concerned rather to correct technical errors and infelicities than to make rhetorical readjustments. There seems never to have been any conscious attempt to restore the punctuation of the manuscripts, and yet both Juliet Grindle and Simon Gatrell have very persuasively argued and demonstrated that, at least in the manuscripts of *Tess of the d'Urbervilles* and *Under the Greenwood Tree,* that punctuation is not only clear and ample but rhetorically sensitive and effective. Dr Grindle shows that the printers for the *Graphic* made well over 3,000 changes to the manuscript punctuation of *Tess,* of which almost half involved the insertion of additional commas.[9]   Even more remarkable, considering the relative length of the two works, is the total of 2,900 punctuation discrepancies between the manuscript of *Under the Greenwood Tree* and the first edition, of which 1,280 involved the addition of commas.[10]   Dr Gatrell's additional demonstration that the compositors varied greatly in the degree of house-styling to which they subjected Hardy's manuscript provides a refreshingly solid piece of evidence in support of the standard theoretical arguments for using the manuscript as copy-text — as, I may add, both Grindle and Gatrell do in the editions that constitute their recent Oxford D.Phil. theses. My own reading of Hardy's manuscripts goes entirely to support the view that they are carefully and deliberately punctuated, and during the process of editing the first volume of Hardy's letters I cannot, off-hand, recall a single instance when editorial intervention was needed to compensate for inadequacies of punctuation — although there were a few instances of periods omitted at the ends of sentences and of unclosed parentheses or quotation marks. Incidentally, Hardy was in his letters and manuscripts an habitual user of double quotation marks, and remained so to the end of his days despite a lifetime's exposure to the single-quote preference of British publishers — including Macmillan in the Wessex Edition.

Hardy's acceptance of the heavier and more rigid punctuation imposed upon his work is not hard to understand. In his early years he must have felt too insecure and too busy to protest; later on it must have seemed unnecessary to worry over details that had been so long established and that were, in any case, technically impeccable. I have already spoken of Hardy's professional acceptance of the contemporary publishing situation, and it is perhaps worth adding that even if he had wanted to consult his manuscripts at the time he was preparing the Wessex Edition he would have been seriously inconvenienced — like succeeding generations of Hardy scholars — by the necessity of travelling to the various libraries on both sides of the Atlantic to which he had presented all but a very few of them just a few months earlier.

I hope I have sufficiently established that by 1912 each of Hardy's texts had gone through long, undramatic processes of erosion and accretion involving many accidents and much house-styling on the part of publishers and printers and, on Hardy's own part, a mixture of determined thoroughness and realistic compromise. The main stages in the transmission of a typical Hardy text are familiar enough: manuscript to serial to first edition (and perhaps a revised first edition), thence to the Osgood, McIlvaine collected edition and so to the Wessex. And these are indeed the points at which the majority of the revisions and corrections were made. But it is necessary to allow also for the various proof-stages preceding each step in the sequence — stages easy to overlook when so few of the proofs survive — and for the possible textual significance of other published forms. It is clear, for example, that Hardy did make revisions — sometimes quite substantial — in some of the cheap one-volume editions of his novels published by Kegan Paul, Sampson Low, Macmillan and others between the first editions and the Osgood, McIlvaine edition; since he used such one-volume editions when preparing copy for some of the Osgood, McIlvaine volumes it is also clear that such revisions fall within the main stream of textual transmission. (It was in the Henry S. King one-volume edition of *A Pair of Blue Eyes,* for example, that Hardy completed his trimming down of the novel's opening chapter, and in the Kegan Paul one-volume edition of *The Return of the Native* that he deleted a reference to a successful eighteenth-century gambler which had been objected to by the gambler's living relatives).[11] Nor can it be automatically assumed that he left untouched the Tauchnitz editions of his novels — he certainly supplied a list of corrections to the Tauchnitz *Two on a Tower* in December 1882[12] — or, for that matter, the Colonial editions published chiefly though not exclusively by Sampson Low and Macmillan — although most of them seem (I speak without benefit of collation) to have been simply impressions or sheets from the current English one-volume editions.

Even the American and occasional Australian serializations of the novels and stories are potential sources of important information. As most of you here will be aware, the lack of international copyright during Hardy's early career often made it necessary for American serialization to be based on the uncorrected proofs of the British serial — which would be rushed across the Atlantic in the hope of anticipating the pirates (I mean the literary ones). In instances where Hardy's original manuscript no longer exists — one thinks especially of "An Indiscretion in the Life of an Heiress" — the American serial text may become valuable for its very preservation of manuscript readings removed from the British serial by Hardy's subsequent revisions.

You may argue that this sounds more like archaeology than editing, and it is true that an editor would be unlikely to adopt readings which Hardy had so immediately rejected. Part of my basic argument here, however, is that errors and oversights could have occurred at almost any stage in the complicated transmission process and become permanently embedded thereafter. Let me take another and more intricate example, and one which an editor could not afford to ignore – that of the "sixpenny" edition of *Far from the Madding Crowd,* published in double-columns and paper covers by Harper & Brothers in 1901, during the period when they were Hardy's principal publishers on both sides of the Atlantic. What is curious here is that the fate of the preface was quite distinct from that of the text proper. It was in this edition that Hardy made the revisions to the original 1895 preface of *Far from the Madding Crowd* that are generally assumed to have been first made in the Uniform Edition, that slightly revised re-issue of the Osgood, McIlvaine edition which Macmillan brought out when they took over from Harper as Hardy's English publishers in 1902. The way in which the 1901 preface revisions became absorbed into the 1902 text is made clear by an entry in Macmillan's Editions Book for 5 September 1902 specifying a print order of 2,000 copies of *Far from the Madding Crowd* "with preface from Harper's Edn."[13] Changes were made in other volumes in 1902, especially in *Jude,* but a general revision with extensive plate-alterations was neither contemplated nor undertaken, and Hardy did not, therefore, transfer the revisions of the actual text of the sixpenny *Far from the Madding Crowd.*

When the time came, almost ten years later, to prepare the Wessex Edition, Hardy was supplied, as we have seen, with a set of the current Uniform impressions, and even if he did not simply forget the corrections to the sixpenny

*Far from the Madding Crowd* he no longer had the copy he had marked up and could therefore have recovered those corrections only by a tedious word-for-word collation. It is possible to speak confidently here since the printer's copy for the sixpenny edition is now deposited, together with the proofs, in the Signet Library, Edinburgh: as one might expect, it is a 1900 Harper impression of the Osgood, McIlvaine text. The corrections were thus not incorporated into the Wessex text — apart from instances of apparently independent duplication — but left stranded within their original paper covers. One amusing consequence — noted, though not explained, by Carl J. Weber[14] — is that Jan Coggan's pinchbeck repeater continues in the first printing of the Wessex Edition to strike one twice in two hours, even though Hardy had spotted and corrected the error in 1901. Whether Hardy made comparable changes to the sixpenny edition of *Tess* prepared and published at approximately the same time I do not know, chiefly because I have never had my hands on a copy: although some 100,000 copies were apparently sold, the cheap format has obviously militated against their survival. It is, however, sufficiently clear that an exhaustive search for potentially relevant forms of the text is as indispensable for the Hardy editor as for any other.

Such a search is likely to be even more tedious and tiresome, but no less necessary, for the years following the first publication of the Wessex Edition. Any editor — anyone at all seriously interested in the transmission of Hardy's text — must absorb, as soon as his stomach will allow, the full implications of Hardy's novels having remained almost continuously in print from their first publication to the present day, and of Hardy himself having lived to enjoy (in his own melancholy fashion) an extremely successful, healthy, active, and extended old age. Not only were some of Hardy's novels published thirty and even forty years before the Wessex Edition, but Hardy lived for almost another sixteen years after April 1912 — years of rich creativity and of almost daily literary housekeeping. As he continued to keep the publishing, translating, dramatizing, and filming of his books under review, so he continued to be concerned with details of their texts: a note on the ending of "The Romantic Adventures of a Milkmaid" is dated September 1927, just four months before he died (at the age of 87, I would remind you); he read the proofs of *Chosen Poems* two months later; and it is possible that he read even later than that the proofs of the posthumously-published *Collected Short Stories*. From time to time he reminded Macmillan of the need to make the changes in the prefaces and texts of the Uniform and Pocket editions which would bring them into line with the Wessex revisions, and in the late 1920s at least some volumes of the Uniform Edition were so revised, re-set, and re-plated. The revised *A Pair of Blue Eyes* of 1927, to take one example, can readily be identified by its reduced total of pages and its inclusion of a more elaborate map — now in the fold-out form which Hardy had wanted for the Wessex Edition itself.

Closer inspection reveals a possible reason for Macmillan's not having made such revisions earlier. The map in the 1927 *A Pair of Blue Eyes* includes several names that were not in the Wessex Edition map of 1912, and the text itself contains numerous revisions that had not been made at that stage. Hardy, in fact, had not stuck to his assertion that he was going through his books "for the last time" in 1912, and his publishers (who may have expected as much) managed by their delay to make all the changes at one economical stroke instead of spreading them expensively over the years. The impetus for Hardy to take yet another look at his texts had come from Macmillan's suggestion, in 1914, for their own *édition de luxe,* and since the Mellstock Edition, as it was called, was delayed by the First World War, Hardy had plenty of time to assemble a list of desired corrections — of which those to *A Pair of Blue Eyes* and the various poetry volumes were by far the most extensive. That list, keyed to the Wessex Edition texts, was submitted in June 1919.

Since the Mellstock Edition was evidently printed with particular care and certainly incorporates authorial revisions subsequent to the 1912 Wessex changes, it might seem, on the face of it, to have some claim to be considered the superior text. Hardy instructed Macmillan, however, that he wished to see no proofs of the prose volumes of the Mellstock Edition other than the pages of *A Pair of Blue Eyes* to which corrections had been made,[15] and with an author as concerned as Hardy for the detail of his text the question of whether or not the proofs of a particular volume were requested and read becomes of critical importance in determining its authority. It was perhaps as a consequence of Hardy's relatively minor involvement in the preparation and publication of the edition that no one noticed until too late that the division of the prose works into categories, a major innovation in the Wessex Edition, had been omitted from the Mellstock altogether. The omission of the Wessex Edition frontispieces, however, appears to have been deliberate. Not surprisingly, the Wessex remained for Hardy the "definitive" text, and he was able in April 1920 to supply his publishers with a list of corrections for a proposed comprehensive re-issue — although *Tess* at least had already been reprinted without corrections as early as 1917. The April 1920 list was apparently identical with the list earlier supplied for the Mellstock Edition, but the records Hardy kept — though remarkable from the very fact of their existence — are a little confusing, and it is possible that some corrections sent for the re-set Mellstock were deemed insufficiently important to justify shifting the existing type of the Wessex Edition (plates seem not to have been made at this time). Even after 1920 Hardy made on his file copies of the Wessex volumes — chiefly on the dust-wrappers — other minor corrections that he stumbled on or had drawn to his attention from time to time; some of these were sent to Macmillan in yet another list in November 1926 and may have been incorporated into the re-set volumes of the Uniform Edition published after that date. They may also have been incorporated into subsequent printings of the Wessex Edition, and collation of those printings, the Mellstock Edition, the post-1926 printings of the Uniform Edition, and Hardy's own records would be necessary to ensure that all his final corrections had been safely gathered in.

In the years 1949-52 Macmillan published the so-called Library Edition, for which the plates seem to have been made by photo-offset from 1920 or post-1920 impressions of the Wessex Edition: it incorporated, that is to say, the 1920 revisions but also a few additional corrections which may or may not have been authorial. Unfortunately, its relatively austere format again excluded the Wessex frontispieces, and after several impressions in the fifties, sixties, and early seventies the plates of the more popular volumes became somewhat worn; even so, its direct relationship to the Wessex Edition made it an extremely useful text for working and teaching purposes. Within just the last few years, however, the Library Edition — or Greenwood Edition, as the later impressions were called — has been entirely replaced by Macmillan's New Wessex Edition, of which the first eight titles appeared in 1974. This is an attractively produced edition, and several of the volumes contain good critical introductions and useful notes. As a series of classroom texts it is of above average quality. But it is well to be aware that its pretensions to textual significance — implicit in its very title — prove on inspection to be somewhat flimsy.

The "Note on the Text" contained in the New Wessex Edition of *Tess of the d'Urbervilles* concludes — like the corresponding note in most of the other volumes — with an assertion that "The text of the present edition is based on

that of the Wessex Edition of 1912."[16]   That statement is
not inaccurate, but there is a world of latitude in the formula
"based on," and it in fact appears that many — if not all —
of the New Wessex volumes were set from late Library or
Greenwood impressions, not from the original Wessex impression of 1912 or even that slightly revised impression of
1920.   In a sense, of course, this places the New Wessex
Edition firmly within a great tradition, since it is precisely
what Hardy himself would have done in the circumstances.
And the procedure does make the volumes more useful than
they might otherwise have been, in that they incorporate
revisions that would have been missed had a return in fact
been made to 1912.   But so broad an interpretation of
"based on" sorts oddly with the elaboration of some of the
textual notes in individual volumes and discourages con-
fidence in the authority of the edition as a whole.   And,
indeed, the New Wessex does prove to contain extensive
house-styling, mostly of a minor nature but not always
so:   it is one thing to omit the periods after abbreviations
such as "Mr." and "Mrs.", another to omit from *Tess* the
structural formulae "End of Phase the First," "End of
Phase the Second," etc.   It also has a good many typographical errors of its own.   No doubt the incidence of
simple error will progressively decrease as corrections are
made in successive printings, but the New Wessex text will
remain that of a house-styled re-setting of late impressions
of the Wessex Edition.   As such, it clearly has strengths as
well as limitations;   what is equally clear, however, is that
it is neither a scholarly edition nor an adequate substitute
for the Wessex Edition itself.   Even its potential usefulness
as a convenient point of reference is compromised by the fact
that its paperback and hardcover forms represent entirely
distinct impositions of the text and are therefore quite
differently paginated.

   This unmaking of the Wessex Edition would not have

mattered so much if the Library/Greenwood volumes had been allowed to remain in print. But the Wessex Edition itself still stands on library shelves, and we may venture to indulge the hope — with more wistfulness, perhaps, than real optimism — that some publisher will celebrate the expiration of Hardy's copyright at the end of next year with a photographic re-issue of the Wessex text of 1912 or 1920, complete with the original frontispieces and the map to which Hardy gave his approval — that in the New Wessex volumes has been depleted not only of its decorative aquatic life but also of a good many of its names in the process of being squeezed into a one-page frame measuring just five and a half inches by three and a half. There may, of course, be copyright difficulties hindering the use of a particular published format, and the prospect is in any case made less likely by that elongated Wessex page to which Hardy himself first drew attention. Our better if longer-term hope must be for scholarly editions of the novels prepared in accordance with the best contemporary standards, and there are encouraging indications of progress in that direction.

But if I have reminded you today of the long and complex developments which comprised the making of the Wessex Edition, I have by the same token drawn attention to the length and complexity of the task of creating something worthy to take its place as the necessary point of scholarly and critical reference, a new "last word in questions of text." Indispensable as the Wessex Edition has been, is now, and will continue to be, it has nonetheless the inherent limitation — as I hope I have sufficiently shown — of being the culmination of an extended process profoundly conditioned at each stage by the circumstances of commercial publishing. By unmaking that process — if I can now apply the second part of my title in a slightly different sense — by unravelling the threads so tightly woven into the Wessex fabric, the textual scholar can learn a great deal about Hardy's working methods and habits of thought, his whole creative cast of mind. If that scholar is also an editor he will have to put the whole thing together again — *re*make it — beginning with the manuscript if it survives (as most of them do) and following through the successive stages of the text to the bitter end not just of Hardy's long life but of that seemingly infinite series of potentially relevant textual forms.

Hardy's novels, as I have said, remained almost continuously in print from the day of their first publication, and in his later years the Uniform and Pocket Editions remained available alongside the more costly Mellstock and various impressions of the Wessex — including that 1926 *Tess* with illustrations by Vivien Gribble which are interesting not only for their own sake but because the model for Tess herself was Gertrude Bugler, who had played the part in the stage version. However exasperating such proliferation may seem, however elusive particular volumes may prove, it is, I suggest, a risky procedure to overlook any of the stages during Hardy's lifetime, and even for two or three years after his death, at which authorial emendations might have been made. And this means not just new editions, nor even re-issues in new formats, but even successive impressions from the same plates and within the same format. Of course, some short cuts can be taken by collating early and late impressions from the same plates — although the possibility of duplicate plates would need to be kept in mind. The fate of the stranded emendations in the sixpenny *Far from the Madding Crowd* is warning enough that the stream of textual transmission does not necessarily follow a smooth and continuous course but can suffer breaks and diversions: indeed, the windings of the Hardyan stream are so tortuous that we ought not to be surprised at the creation of an occasional bayou.

The editorial task thus envisaged would be long, wearisome, and largely mechanical. But not wholly so. Peter Shillingsburg has already insisted that the second thoughts of authors are not inevitably the best, and in Hardy's case we are often dealing with the umpteenth thoughts. Hardy himself made much this point when he told Frederic Harrison, just about the time when he was revising the sixpenny *Far from the Madding Crowd,* that there was perhaps something in the novel which he could not have put there if he had been older.[17]  While accepting the point in principle, however, I still feel that an editor would need strong grounds for rejecting the final revisions of an author such as Hardy who retained his creative powers literally to the day of his death — when he is said to have dictated, no doubt from memory, two sharp and savage epitaphs on George Moore and G. K. Chesterton.  But I have been arguing throughout that each of Hardy's many revisions was done in terms of the immediately preceding form of the text — that it was always, therefore, a fixing up rather than a radical reconsideration (though he did go back to the manuscript when restoring to *Tess* and *The Mayor of Casterbridge* passages which had at first been omitted from the published forms).  It is also clear that he made or accepted under pressures of various kinds a good many changes that he would not have made independently. In response to the moral — which generally meant commercial — sensitivities of editors he made bowdlerizations in his serial texts which for reasons of caution or oversight or sheer weariness were not always restored in the book form.  He also revised the book form itself, on occasion, to meet objections made by reviewers to particular words or passages. A well-known instance is the scene in Chapter 6 of *Jude the Obscure* in which Arabella attracts Jude's attention by throwing at him "the characteristic part of a barrow-pig." Many of the hostile reviewers of the novel seized particularly on this scene, and when Macmillan took over the Osgood, McIlvaine edition in 1902 Hardy took the opportunity to tone down some of the references to the doubly offensive offal. Despite the additional authority given to those changes by their subsequent absorption into the Wessex Edition, an editor who wanted to restore the earlier readings — as has already been done in one paperback text of the novel[18] — would certainly be on strong ground. My personal decision, however — in the midst of this clash of principles and authorities — would, I think, be to stand by the Wessex reading, not dogmatically, just because it was Hardy's final choice, but because I happen to think that his revisions, taken in their entirety, are aesthetically superior, making for a more consistent characterization of Jude and Arabella, a more credible sequence of events, and an enhancement of the scene's predominantly comic tone.

There is also the question — should anyone be rash enough to ask it — of the many changes made in successive revisions, chiefly those for the Osgood, McIlvaine and Wessex editions, to details of dialect and topography. Since these aren't always consistent in their direction either from one revision to the next, or even within a single revision, it might be possible to argue with some of them. The danger involved, however, in rejecting a late emendation of this kind would be that of possibly suppressing an item of autobiographical significance, a reading that Hardy might have adopted from the very beginning if he had felt free to do so: the late changes Hardy made to *A Pair of Blue Eyes* were almost all designed to consolidate and emphasize the book's connection with the setting and circumstances of his own courtship of his first wife, and it is entirely possible that late changes in other novels — *Under the Greenwood Tree,* perhaps, or *Far from the Madding Crowd* — incorporate details of remembered scenes or places or, more especially, phrases or sayings associated in Hardy's memory with the real-life originals of his fictional figures.

Clearly there is no such thing as pure editing. The editor, who must necessarily start by being a bibliographer, must become in some measure a critic and even a biographer too, even while thinking of himself all the while as a galley-slave. So burdened, he could be forgiven for reflecting how much simpler it would all have been if Hardy had carried out the scheme he somewhat whimsically confided to Henry Newbolt in 1906:

> I am thinking of approximating to the methods of the early ages, writing my books on parchment, & lending them round; or what would be a somewhat more practical method, getting type-written copies of my next book made under my eye, & supplying them to the public on application by post to the author, with postal order.[19]

The simplicity would of course have been illusory — an editor would presumably have had to collate each typed copy with every other — and the procedure would, to say the least, have rendered Hardy notably less prolific — especially if he had ended up packing the parcels. The great and good thing about commercial publishing, however much we may complain about its misdeeds, is that it does get books published, and hence, directly or indirectly, provides each of us here not only with a living but with a context which makes that living worthwhile. Macmillan's Wessex Edition was a magnificent achievement for author and publisher alike, and it can be faulted only when measured against those ideal standards with which, as scholars, we must always be concerned. There is little wrong, for that matter, with Macmillan's New Wessex Edition, except that it makes through its title a larger claim for the closeness of its relationship to its great ancestor than the adducible evidence will really sustain.

## NOTES

1  Letter to Sir Frederick Macmillan, 12 October 1910 (British Library).

2  Letter to Sir Frederick Macmillan, 10 January 1912 (British Library).

3  Letter to Sir Frederick Macmillan, 2 April 1912 (British Library).

4  Letter to Macmillan & Co., 25 October 1911 (British Library).

5  Letter to Daniel Macmillan, 5 February 1912 (British Library).

6  Letter to Daniel Macmillan, 15 February 1912 (British Library).

7  Letter to Sydney Cockerell, 4 May 1912 (Frederick B. Adams).

8  Richard Little Purdy, *Thomas Hardy: A Bibliographical Study*, Oxford, Clarendon Press, 1968, p. 286.

9  Juliet Grindle, "A Critical Edition of Thomas Hardy's *Tess of the d'Urbervilles*," unpub. D. Phil. thesis, Oxford, 1974, p. lxx.

10  Simon Gatrell, "A Critical Edition of Thomas Hardy's Novel *Under the Greenwood Tree*," unpub. D. Phil. thesis, Oxford, 1973, pp. lxiv-lxv.

11  See Richard L. Purdy and Michael Millgate, ed., *The Collected Letters of Thomas Hardy*, I, Oxford, Clarendon Press, 1978, p. 64.

12  Letter to Hardy from Christian Bernhard Tauchnitz, 15 December 1882 (Dorset County Museum).

13  British Library, Add. Mss. 55914, p. 94.

14  Carl J. Weber, *Hardy and the Lady from Madison Square*, Waterville, Maine, Colby College Press, 1952, p. 233.

15  Letter to Sir Frederick Macmillan, 18 June 1919 (British Library).

16  *Tess of the d'Urbervilles*, London, Macmillan, 1974, p. 471 (paperback text).

17  Letter to Frederic Harrison, 29 July 1901 (University of Texas, Austin).

18  *Jude the Obscure,* ed. F. R. Southerington, Indianapolis, Bobbs-Merrill, 1972.

19  Letter to Henry Newbolt, 4 November 1906 (University of Texas, Austin). I am grateful to the trustees of the estate of Miss E. A. Dugdale for permission to quote from this letter and from the letter to S. C. Cockerell of 4 May 1912 in advance of their publication in the *Collected Letters.*

# On Editing Zola's Fiction

## Clive Thomson

When I first became interested in the problems related to the editing of Emile Zola's novels,[1] one important fact was immediately clear to me. Although much editing has indeed been done and at least one good practical edition of Zola's major novels does exist, the editors themselves have never taken the time to explain or justify at length their editorial decisions or the theoretical presuppositions of their work. It is true to say that existing editions are based on an empirical approach[2] and that we Zola editors are still a very long way from the stage reached by several editors of American fiction.[3] Despite a few isolated efforts in France,[4] material bibliography is still dominated by Anglo-American scholars. Progress made, especially in the United States, has no equivalent in France.[5]

By way of preface to the main development of my paper, let me say that Zola scholars seem to have had one of two attitudes toward the subject of editing Zola's fiction. Very few articles on textual problems in Zola's work or on the author's habits of revision have been produced. Those articles which have been written usually begin with an embarrassed apology for dealing with such a tedious and unimportant subject.[6] That is one attitude. The other is that there really isn't much to be said about the question of establishing the texts of Zola's novels because the problems are simple and straightforward.[7] The general purpose of my paper is to explain why such attitudes are both unjustified and erroneous.

I have divided my paper into three parts. In the first section, I would like to describe briefly the textual material available for Zola's novels and to make a short survey of the editions which have been published, as well as the principles upon which they are based. Secondly, I shall try to define a few of the central textual problems one faces in editing Zola's fiction. I hope that some discussion will arise out of this section of my paper. And, finally, I shall ask the question: do we really need a new edition of Zola's novels, and, if so, of what kind? My presentation is, therefore, a kind of "état présent" on the editing of Emile Zola's novels.[8] If I accepted the invitation to speak at this editorial conference, it was primarily because I felt it useful to undertake this kind of study. No one has bothered to write such a paper before, not even, as I have said, the major textual editors in the field.

Let me outline summarily the nature of the textual materials available. Complete manuscripts exist for twenty-five of the thirty-one Zola novels;[9] five others have been lost (these include all of the earliest novels), and one is incomplete (that of La Fortune des Rougon). Twenty-nine of the thirty-one novels were published serially before appearing in book form. Corrected proofs exist for eleven novels. Corrected page copy has been preserved in the case of six novels. The availability of so much material is a great advantage to the textual critic, but it does not mean that there are no problems.

In the case of *La Confession de Claude,* Zola's first novel, there is no manuscript, no serial publication, no corrected proof. Copy-text clearly has to be the first edition (1865). For *La Terre* (1887), however, things are more complicated. The Bibliothèque Nationale in Paris possesses the manuscript for the novel, corrected proofs from the serial publication, and corrected proofs from the first edition printing. But neither the serial version nor the first edition follow exactly the corrected proofs. This means that Zola might have corrected yet a second set of proofs at each stage. It is very difficult to know if this was the case, and I shall come back to the problem later on.

It should be obvious from the preceding remarks that the point at which Zola corrected proofs is a significant moment in the genetic history of his novels, in contrast to what some critics have frequently implied. If scholars have tended to ignore this part of the Zola genesis, it is probably for one of two reasons. In the first place, potential editors are easily discouraged when presented with the tedious task of so much collating. Some novels went through dozens of editions and impressions in the author's lifetime. And, secondly, critics have been much more interested in examining the so-called "dossiers préparatoires" or preparatory dossiers which exist for twenty-six of the thirty-one novels. As most of you probably know, Zola undertook a lengthy period of research on the subject to be dealt with, before sitting down to write the novel itself. This pre-manuscript material is composed of preliminary sketches of the plot, brief outlines of the characters' personalities and histories, reading notes taken from secondary sources, general and detailed plans of the plot, and various other kinds of notes. For a novel like *Germinal,* for example, there are 953 pages of pre-manuscript notes. For *Paris,* the third of the *Trois Villes* trilogy, there are some 1300 pages of pre-manuscript material.

All of Zola's novels were published during his lifetime,

with the exception of *Vérité*, which appeared shortly after the writer's death. Only four novels have been the subject of complete critical editions: three in the form of theses *(Paris, Fécondité, Travail)*, and one in published form *(Le Ventre de Paris)*.[10] The reading public and scholars have at their disposal, then, very few scholarly editions.[11] If we look briefly at some of the practical or popular commercial editions, we shall see that they have the usual advantages and disadvantages of such editions.

Two complete editions of the novels have come out since 1960. Henri Guillemin directed the first of these (1960-62) in twenty-four volumes (Editions Rencontre), and Henri Mitterand (Professor at the Université de Paris-Vincennes) was responsible for the second (Cercle du Livre Précieux), as part of the *Oeuvres complètes* in fifteen volumes (published between 1966 and 1969). Guillemin's edition has no critical apparatus and represents a minimal editorial effort. Mitterand's version of the novels is much more interesting and useful since it contains an introduction and textual annotations for each novel. These introductions and notes are limited to discussion of genetic and historical material plus some literary commentary. Although Mitterand is careful to indicate what he uses as copy-text for his edition, the reader will not find a statement of editorial procedures or a presentation of variants. This edition goes no further, as far as establishing the texts of the novels is concerned, than Mitterand's own earlier Pléiade edition of the Rougon-Macquart series, which I shall discuss more fully in a moment. Like all of the practical editions presently under discussion, the Cercle du Livre Précieux version has unfortunately been standardized in matters of punctuation, spelling, and paragraphing. This was done, I assume, in order to conform to publishing house standards, and does not represent what the editor would ideally have chosen to do.

Two editions of Zola's major and most lastingly successful

series of novels, the *Rougon-Macquart*, have been produced. Pierre Cogny directed the first of these, in six volumes for the Seuil publishing house (1969-70). This edition, like the Guillemin edition, has no critical apparatus, and its editorial commentary consists only of a brief historical or literary introduction to each novel. Cogny admits that his intention was not to introduce new material but rather to rely on Mitterand's Pléiade edition of these same novels.

Professor Mitterand's edition of the *Rougon-Macquart* sequence, published in the Bibliothèque de la Pléiade by Gallimard (1960-67), in five volumes, is based on the following general principles: copy-text is supposedly the last one to have been corrected by Zola, in most cases the first edition. One finds in the critical apparatus a selection of variants from serial publication and from any existing corrected proofs, although the editor chooses not to present manuscript variants. This edition is really a monument in Zola scholarship and its limitations are only those imposed by the publishing house where it was produced. Professor Mitterand's principal interest was not so much in the establishing of the texts of the novels as in elucidating Zola's compositional procedures at an earlier stage in the creative process. Each novel is followed by a brilliant analysis of Zola's preparatory notes, sketches, and plans. As far as the textual editing is concerned, the limitations of the Pléiade are as follows: we have only a *selection* of variants from pre-first edition published versions, rather than all variants from all pre-first edition texts, including the manuscript, which would, of course, be included in a thorough critical edition. Since Professor Mitterand does not give all variants, it is impossible to know exactly how many times or in what sequence Zola corrected his proofs.[12]

The proof-correcting stage of the Zola genesis remains, therefore, an area of mystery and speculation. As I suggested a moment ago, as far as *La Terre* is concerned, there is some doubt as to whether or not the author corrected one or two

sets of proofs for each of the serial and first edition publications. There is also the problem of deciding who was
responsible, Zola or a compositor, for variants which appear
in editions subsequent to the first. It is generally believed
that Zola stopped correcting his text with the first edition.
Only a very careful collating of all editions published during
the writer's lifetime would clarify this difficulty.

Let me conclude this first part of my paper by discussing
rapidly the pocket-book editions of Zola's novels. In some
ways, they are paradoxically the least satisfying and the most
interesting. The "Livre de Poche" series is the opposite of a
complete scholarly edition. There are no introductions, no
critical apparatus, and no mention of what is being used as
copy-text. The Garnier-Flammarion publishers have put out
in pocket-book format eighteen Zola novels. The text of
each novel is preceded by an introduction, usually written
by a well-known Zola scholar. This is the most valuable part
of the series. However, textual editing is somewhat haphazard.
In some cases, but not all, the reader learns what is being
used as copy-text. No variants are given. The Gallimard
publishing house has recently also begun issuing Zola's novels
in pocket-book form. To date, only two have appeared: *La
Bête humaine* and *Nana.*[13] Procedures here are similar to
the ones used in the Garnier-Flammarion series.[14]

I would now like to describe briefly what is known at the
present time about Zola's habits of revision[15] and, in the
process, point out those areas where our knowledge is weak.
I shall also be able to dispel some popular myths about this
stage in the Zola genesis.

It is a widespread belief that Zola took little interest in his
work at the proof-correcting stage. Zola himself professed
a great dislike for this activity and even admitted that he
found it very painful to reread his own novels.[16] He claimed
that as soon as he had finished one book, he would rush on
to the next, trying as best he could to forget the one just

completed. It is also generally held that Zola limited his emendations to minor aspects of style. My own examination of only some of the manuscript material available does not support any of these assumptions.

In fact, Zola's habits of revision and adjustment evolved tremendously over the course of his long career and one simple description of what he did is not possible. Let me try to elucidate some of his most characteristic procedures. At the beginning of his literary career, when he was working on *La Fortune des Rougon* (1869-71), Zola can be seen to modify his plot, to add new characters, and to change names, even at the moment of proof-correction. This is due to the fact that he was enlarging the general scope of the *Rougon-Macquart* cycle while he was still in the middle of writing *La Fortune des Rougon,* the first novel in the series. By the time he was composing the *Trois Villes* trilogy (1894-98), modifications of his texts at the proof stage were almost always of a stylistic nature.

Furthermore, it is clear that Zola was never satisfied with his novels until the last proofs went to the printer. Modifications are continuous in all of his novels and their greater or lesser quantity, depending on the novel, is usually determined quite simply by how pressed for time the author was. In *La Curée,* it was only when Zola was correcting proofs for the first edition that he decided to call the hero Saccard. In a similar way, the character Larcher, in *Le Ventre de Paris,* becomes Verlaque as Zola is adjusting first edition proofs. Similar examples could be cited for most novels.

Zola was in the habit of sending his novels to the printer chapter by chapter, as he finished writing them, and without waiting until there was a complete manuscript. He often corrected proofs for serial publication, and sometimes even for first editions, while he was still in the middle of writing a novel. In fact, he was obliged on several occasions to request that serial publication be slowed down as he was getting behind. In the case of *L'Assommoir*, serial publication was stopped, partly because Zola ran out of copy for the compositor. In later novels, when Zola was more organized in his working habits, no such accidents seem to have occurred. However, it is still possible to find evidence in his working notes of proofs being corrected before the novels were completed. Such is the case with *Paris*. Scholars have tended to ignore the influence of such a procedure on the structure and style of Zola's novels, and until a complete critical edition exists an investigation of this subject will not be possible. Suffice it to say that much remains to be learned about this stage in the creative process.

Let me now go on to talk about some of the more interesting textual problems to which I referred earlier. In order to be brief, I shall be obliged to illustrate my remarks with only a few random examples from the textual material. The merits and defects of proceeding in this way simply reflect the fact that I am dealing with a new field of research in Zola studies.

As stated a moment ago, the task of assembling the textual elements (manuscripts, corrected proofs, etc.) to be dealt with is not a difficult one. Zola, in whom the collecting instinct was developed to an extreme degree, tried to keep in his possession every scrap of his own manuscript matter, not to mention every letter or note that he received.[17] There is little problem in working out what text to use as copytext: with few exceptions, it is usually the first published edition. Difficulties arise, however, when one begins to establish the texts of the novels. I pointed out a few moments ago that corrected proofs and corrected page copy exist for certain of Zola's novels but not by any means for all of them. In the case of the *Trois Villes,* for example, there are no known corrected proofs. However, it is beyond doubt that the author did see and alter proofs submitted to him before serial and first edition publications. Zola talks of these proofs in his personal correspondence. But it is extremely hard to know who was responsible, a compositor or Zola himself, for the variants which appear. In my own edition of *Paris,* I show an average of three or four variants per page, of which the vast majority are of the accidental kind. Substantive changes can be attributed to Zola with little hesitation, but the accidental ones pose problems precisely because the writer was very concerned about matters of punctuation, capitalization, and spelling. Whereas many nineteenth-century novelists tended to be quite unconcerned about this kind of detail, Zola was very different. I have no concrete solution to this problem, but my feeling at the moment is that one would have to collate many novels before being able to attribute responsibility for variants to Zola or to his publisher. If one were to record all the accidental variants for several novels (or for all novels, ideally), patterns would undoubtedly emerge, and in the light of evidence from the corrected proofs that we do have, one could convincingly establish two categories of variants — those for which Zola was responsible and those which came from the printer.

There is another problem related to the one just outlined. At the time of serial publication, many of Zola's novels were expurgated. The scene from *Germinal* in which Maigrat is castrated by the wives of the miners does not appear in the *Gil Blas* version, nor do some other passages. Similarly, many sexual references in *L'Assommoir* and *Pot-Bouille* are omitted from the newspaper publications. It was the author's custom to reinsert such passages when correcting proofs for his first editions, so that, in some cases, the first edition text resembles the manuscript text more closely than it does the serial text. Zola did not always reestablish every expurgated section, probably because there was not enough time to do so. The textual editor is constantly in the position of having to decide, often on very little evidence, what text to reproduce in his edition.

A third problem concerns the filiation or relationship of the three texts that one usually finds for each Zola novel: manuscript, serial text, first edition text. The chronological sequence in which the texts were produced is often straight-forward: manuscript first, followed by the serial, then the first edition. The printer of the first edition would have the serial text at his disposal and would set his type from it. The textual filiation can be illustrated as follows:

However, contrary to what is generally understood, the situation is not always so simple. In the case of *Son Excellence Eugène Rougon,* the textual relationships can be presented as follows:

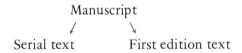

This is to say that the typesetters for the serial publication *and* the first edition had access to the manuscript. There is at least one more documented procedure:

This schema represents the way in which the printing of *Le*

*Docteur Pascal* took place. Zola gave his manuscript to his book publisher first, in stages, and the book publisher in turn gave his printed text to the newspaper, *La Revue hebdomadaire.* The question I would ask is this: would it be necessary to distinguish these filiations in a complete critical edition, and if so, how could they be presented typographically?

At the beginning of my paper, I said that I would answer the question as to whether or not we need a new edition of Zola's novels. The answer is obvious: a complete scholarly edition is what is required. Unfortunately, for several reasons (among them, economic difficulties in the publishing industry and a seeming lack of interest in textual criticism on the part of Zola scholars), such an edition is not likely to become available in the near future. However, I think it useful, even at this point, to put forward some suggestions for future textual editors.

A new edition should be based on a coherent textual theory, in which methodological presuppositions are not left undefined. The unsystematically empirical and positivistic approach, which characterizes our existing editions, must be replaced by one based on a modern textual theory, and by that I mean one which would take into account recent research in fields such as semiotics and discourse analysis. A textual editor should first define what he means by "text," since the way in which he goes about his editing and sets up his edition will be determined by his conception of such basics. In the past, since editors have most often been literary historians, on whose shoulders nineteenth-century traditions weighed heavily, the principal areas of textual concern have been in exploring authorial intention, in situating texts in their historical context, and in establishing the so-called definitive text. The stages through which a text passed, from manuscript to serial publication to first edition, were viewed as a progression toward some kind of ideal text.[18]   A more modern approach would consider the manuscript, the serial text, and the first edition text as independent documents, each with its own specific characteristics.   It would, of course, be part of the editor's duties to establish the texts of the novels, but it would also be so much more interesting to study how the text of a novel is transformed at each stage.[19]   Such a study should be part of an introduction, and not hidden away at the end of the book in an appendix, as is the custom with these matters.   Because Zola often — but not always — limited his proof modifications to those of a stylistic kind, critics have very frequently talked only about variants as they affect the sentence.   But such stylistic analyses are usually too narrow in scope:  variants should be discussed as they affect the whole work, not just a paragraph or a sentence.   One should ask the question:  what does the change in a single passage reveal about the whole work?

In conclusion, let me outline some of the ways, both direct and indirect, in which those interested in Zola would benefit from a new critical edition.   First of all, we would learn something about an important stage in the genesis of novels. Because Zola spent so much time modifying his texts between manuscript and first edition and did it systematically throughout his whole career, it is clear that this is an essential part of the creative process.   We would also increase our knowledge of the printing industry in nineteenth-century France.  Little is known about how texts were typeset or how books were physically produced.[20]   In Zola's case, we have no detailed study of his relationship with his publisher, Georges Charpentier.   There is yet another way in which a critical edition could be useful.  I said earlier that Zola's novels were expurgated for serial publication.  A systematic study of the kinds of passages deleted would probably reveal interesting aspects of the bourgeois mentality of the period.   In yielding to social pressures, real or imagined, publishers altered their texts accordingly and thus can be seen to reveal much about the society in which they lived.

I would like to close with a quotation from Philip Gaskell which contains a notion already underlined in my paper, but one which bears repeating: "A textual editor is nothing if he is not a literary critic. . . . Textual bibliography is based on the union of literary judgment with bibliographical expertise."[21]

NOTES

1 As the title implies, my paper deals with Zola's novels and not his other fictional writings, such as the short stories. An excellent *complete* critical edition of Zola's *Contes et nouvelles* was published by Roger Ripoll in 1976 (Bibliothèque de la Pléiade, Gallimard).

2 Wallace Kirsop suggests that such an approach is characteristic of textual criticism in France: "D'où, sans doute, un goût de la discussion théorique chez les bibliographes anglo-saxons, qui semblent fuir l'empirisme qui est devenu caractéristique de la tradition française" (*Bibliographie matérielle et critique textuelle: vers une collaboration*, Paris, Lettres Modernes, 1970, pp. 27-28).

3 I refer, of course, to such theoretical documents as the following: *Statement of Editorial Principles and Procedures: A Working Manual for Editing Nineteenth-Century American Texts* (revised edition), New York, Modern Language Association of America, 1972.

4 Roger Laufer, one of the few material bibliographers in France, has published an important study: *Introduction à la textologie*, Paris, Larousse (Collection L), 1972. Jean Bellemin-Noël, who, like Laufer, teaches at the Université de Paris-Vincennes, has written a fascinating book on the manuscripts of the poet Milosz: *Le Texte et l'avant-texte*, Paris, Larousse (Collection L), 1972.

5 An exception is Louis Hay, of the Centre National de la Recherche Scientifique in Paris, who is currently working on the manuscripts of Henri Heine. Hay discusses his research in a paper (to be published shortly) given at the University of Toronto colloquium,

*De l'avant-texte au texte,* held on November 13 and 14, 1976.

6   John Lapp, in a way that is typical of other Zola scholars, makes this statement:   "It would have been possible, in addition, to compare for every novel three versions:   the manuscript, the printed 'feuilleton', and the book, but I do not believe that such a gigantic undertaking would produce any more significant results than those I have already observed" ("On Zola's Habits of Revision," *Modern Language Notes,* 83, [1958], 611.) The fact of the matter is that Lapp's discoveries, as discussed in his article, are of considerable interest to the textual critic, and his tendency to down-play them is regrettable.

7   Pierre Cogny precedes his Seuil edition of the *Rougon-Macquart* novels with the following remark:   "Les problèmes textuels sont relativement simples en ce qui concerne notre auteur. Les chercheurs ont en effet à leur disposition trois états pour chaque roman du cycle:  1. Les manuscrits . . . 2. Le texte du feuilleton . . . 3. L'édition originale . . ." (Volume I, p. 12).

8   As far as surveys of the literary and historical dimension of Zola's work are concerned, students and teachers have been well served. Two fine recent examples of this kind of study are: Dorothy Speirs, "Etat présent des études sur *Les Quatre Evangiles,*" in *Les Cahiers naturalistes,* 48 (1974), 215-35;   Robert Lethbridge, "Twenty Years of Zola Studies (1956-1975)," *French Studies,* 31 (1977), 281-93.

9   Zola's novelistic output consists of the following:  five early novels *(La Confession de Claude, Le Voeu d'une morte, Les Mystères de Marseille, Thérèse Raquin, Madeleine Férat),* the twenty-volume *Rougon-Macquart* cycle, the *Trois Villes (Lourdes, Rome, Paris)* and the *Quatre Evangiles* (four novels were projected but only three had been completed when Zola died unexpectedly in 1902: *Fécondité, Travail, Vérité).*   Most manuscript material for Zola's novels is located at the Bibliothèque Nationale in Paris. Manuscripts for the *Trois Villes* are at the Bibliothèque Méjanes, Aix-en-Provence. The manuscript for *Nana* is at the Pierpont Morgan Library in New York.   Harvard University Library possesses corrected proofs for *Pot-Bouille.*  The New York Public Library has corrected proofs for

*La Joie de Vivre* and *Germinal,* and the library of the University of California at Los Angeles holds corrected proofs for *Le Docteur Pascal.*

10  Clive Thomson, *Edition critique de 'Paris' d'Emile Zola, avec introduction historique et étude génétique* (thesis, University of Toronto, 1976); David Baguley, *'Les Quatre Evangiles'. 'Fécondité'. Edition critique, étude, notes, variantes* (thesis, Université de Nancy, 1969); Dorothy Speirs, *Edition critique de 'Travail' d'Emile Zola* (thesis, University of Toronto, 1977). The only published complete critical edition of a Zola novel is Marc Baroli, ed., *Le Ventre de Paris,* Paris, Minard, 1969.

11  For the distinction between "practical" and "scholarly" editing, see Fredson Bowers' article in Fredson Bowers and Charles Hinman, *Two Lectures on Editing: Shakespeare and Hawthorne,* Columbus, Ohio, Ohio State University Press, 1969, pp. 26-27.

12  Professor Mitterand's description of an ideal critical edition is as follows: "Nous ne nous dissimulons pas qu'une édition critique intégrale devrait reproduire la totalité des transformations du texte, dans l'ordre exact de la création, depuis la première ligne de *l'Ebauche* jusqu'à la dernière ligne de l'édition définitive" (*Les Rougon-Macquart,* volume 4, éd. Mitterand, Paris, Bibliothèque de la Pléiade, Gallimard, 1966, p. 1335).

13  Both novels, published in 1977 in the *Folio* series, are edited and annotated by H. Mitterand, who states that copy-text for *La Bête humaine* was the text of the Pléiade edition. One would rather have expected the first edition to be used.

14  Yet another pocket series of Zola's novels is projected, thus testifying to the increasing demand for Zola's fiction on the part of the popular reading public. Colette Becker is currently preparing an edition of *Germinal* in the Garnier "jaune" series.

15  The few relevant studies which have been written are: John Lapp, article cited in note 6 above; Elliott M. Grant, "The Composition of *La Curée,*" *Romanic Review,* 45 (1954), pp. 29-44; David Baguley, "Les Variantes de *Fécondité,*" in *'Fécondité' d'Emile Zola: roman à thèse, évangile, mythe,* Toronto, University of

Toronto Press, 1973, pp. 230-32; D. Speirs and C. Thomson, theses cited in note 10 above; H. Mitterand's edition of the *Rougon-Macquart*, passim.

16 "Je ne puis me relire, cela me comble de tristesse"; "J'oublie très bien mes oeuvres, que je ne rouvre jamais" (R. J. Niess, ed., *Emile Zola's Letters to J. Van Santen Kolff*, St Louis, Washington University Press, 1940, pp. 46, 48).

17 The Bibliothèque Nationale in Paris possesses some 5,000 letters received by Zola during his lifetime. The family heirs have in their private archives an even greater quantity.

18 Bernard Weinberg devotes part of the following article to this idea: "Editing Balzac: A Problem in Infinite Variation," in J. M. Robson, ed., *Editing Nineteenth-Century Texts*, Toronto, University of Toronto Press, 1966, pp. 60-76. Fredson Bowers puts the conception of literary genesis in rather more ideological terms: "Though a poem, like a man, may stand rejoicing in finished maturity, we must surely understand it with superior intimacy if we have watched its growth and seen its perfection in the very act of shaping" (*Textual and Literary Criticism*, Cambridge, Cambridge University Press, 1959, p. 17).

19 For another attempt to define a modern approach to textual editing, see James Thorpe's interesting essay in *The Task of an Editor*, University of California at Los Angeles, William Andrews Clark Memorial Library, 1969.

20 See Fredson Bowers, "Old Wine in New Bottles: Problems of Machine Printing," in J. M. Robson, ed., *Editing Nineteenth-Century Texts*, Toronto, University of Toronto Press, 1967, pp. 9-36.

21 Philip Gaskell, *A New Introduction to Bibliography*, Oxford, Clarendon Press, 1972, p. 338.

# Aesthetic Implications of Authorial Excisions:
## Examples from Nathaniel Hawthorne, Mark Twain, and Stephen Crane

## Hershel Parker

For all the great amount of editing and theorizing about editing in the last decades, it sometimes seems that we have done very little thinking about concepts we use every day. One of these is the notion of "author's final intentions," a phrase that has become formulaic — and oversimplified — among the followers of W. W. Greg.[1] Inherent in the notion is the belief that when an author revises he always improves; an editor is not to reason why a change was made — it is enough that the author made it, and it should be introduced forthwith into a critical text. The dogma that "last is best" has led some editors to overlook strong biographical evidence that last was not even authorial, much less best. And the dogma that an editor must establish and preserve what the author finally wanted has led scholars and critics to speak harshly of anyone who thinks about printing an earlier form or forms of a text. The upshot of the dominance of Greg's theory, particularly as applied by Fredson Bowers, is that very few people are bothering to think about the various possible points during or after composition at which writers might have the fullest sense of their intentions, and about what actually happens when authors revise a completed work.  When they revise, do authors often have a firm sense of their earlier intentions at the time they wrote a given passage or at the time they first completed the work as a whole?  How often do authors ever gain a comprehensive sense of the new functions that old material must take on in any extensive revision?  How often are authors aware that the excision of one passage must alter the functions of the part which is not excised?  My hunch, as far as excisions are concerned, is that writers rarely know what they are doing when they merely excise — that is, when they merely cut passages from a completed work without rethinking and rewriting the whole.

It is not fair to blame the failure to ask such questions on Greg and Bowers — certainly not on Greg, who was tentative and exploratory rather than dogmatic.  As Bruce Harkness long ago pointed out,[2] professors of English have never thought that words matter very much, especially in long fiction: there are so many of them, after all — how can a few be important?  The academic — Philistine — view which Harkness identified is best summed up by the story about Theodore Dreiser's comment on someone's massive cuts in one of his books: "What's 50,000 words among friends?" When the Philistines get around to writing literary essays they find that the New Criticism has bequeathed them a magic word for dealing with authorial excisions — "pace"; excisions in a work of fiction are always good because they speed up the pace.  Even a work as short as *The Red Badge of Courage,* critics say, was much improved by the pace-quickening excisions made for the 1895 Appleton edition.  Few critics prove strong enough to resist the temptation to say that

"Hawthorne was wise to delete . . ." or "Stephen Crane ultimately saw how distracting the passage was" — situations in which Critic pats Author on the head, thereby affirming his own superiority to the Author's earlier self, if not the later one.

In this paper I want to look at some examples from Nathaniel Hawthorne, Mark Twain, and Stephen Crane which suggest that when writers excise — when they merely delete passages without rethinking and rewriting extensive parts of the book — they very often do more harm than good. But first I want to start by patting an author on the head for making some wise excisions. That's wrong: nobody, not even a critic, would dare to pat Henry David Thoreau on the head. I am bringing in a reference to *Walden,* although it is not exactly fiction, because Joseph McElrath has recently posed some good questions about responsibility for the many large excisions that were made between the last stage of the surviving manuscript and the surviving proofs.[3] McElrath's curiosity was aroused by the many passages printed in the *Annotated Walden* but not present in the first edition.[4] My impression from a quick look at the manuscript in the Huntington Library is that the excisions were Thoreau's doing and that he knew what he was up to. In general, the excised passages seem to have been digressive to begin with. Some of them begin with the damning words "By the way" or contain in themselves other admission that they were digressive. Some of the passages were originally interlineations, and sometimes at the next rewriting these interlineations were copied currently into the text as an integral part of the passage into which they were inserted, only to be cut out again still later: apparently Thoreau remembered or felt them as interpolations even when there was nothing on the page to reveal them as such. Most of the excisions seem due to Thoreau's careful attempt to restrain the digressive tendency that had been given such free play in *A Week on the Concord and Merrimack Rivers.* Often enough he seems to have assimilated the essence of a deleted passage into what he retained, reusing the material in the first edition so that a strange redundancy would result if an editor ever spliced in the deleted words.

Thoreau's excisions in the *Walden* material were part of a cautious final polishing which took place before or during the final copying out of the manuscript, or else just after it was copied out. They were not excisions made in a work which had already been finished or actually published in a different form. Now I want to look at two instances in which Nathaniel Hawthorne indulged himself in just such post-publication deletion. In both cases, "The Gentle Boy" and "The Hall of Fantasy," the Ohio State edition prints the shorter, later version, and does so with no discussion at all of the possible issues, aesthetic or otherwise; a brief note to the Textual Commentary directs the reader to other volumes for a statement of editorial principles.[5] The governing principle, of course, is that an author's final intentions are always valid and must be respected by the editor of a critical edition.

"The Gentle Boy" was first published in the *Token* for 1832. Hawthorne came to feel that it was the product of an "imperfect and ill-wrought conception."[6] Perhaps it was. Perhaps some of the historical passages were not imaginatively assimilated into the tale. In any case, the revisions for *Twice-Told Tales* (1837) consisted mainly of cuts in such passages. But Hawthorne did not reconceive the story — he just hacked away at it. Despite the deletions, his historian's impulse persists in the 1837 version, although less conspicuously and more erratically than before. And the text is left less coherent, as, for example, when the motivation for the Puritans' cruelty toward the Quakers is drastically reduced. The damage occurs in small instances as well, as when a deletion of an early description of the Pearsons' furnishings weakens an otherwise moving section which was designed to recapitulate the deleted passage. We learn in the 1837 text that the "furniture of peace" has disappeared along with "the implements of war," but that is the first we have heard of either in this shorter version. "But the Holy Book remained," we are still told in 1837, although the earlier mention of the Bible has been removed.

An even clearer example of slapdash authorial excision — and mechanical textual editing — is provided by Hawthorne's "The Hall of Fantasy," published first in *The Pioneer* (February, 1843) then revised for inclusion in *Mosses from an Old Manse* (1846). The main difference between the texts is that the *Mosses* version lacks long passages in which Hawthorne depicted some of his literary contemporaries by name. This is the way one section appears in *Mosses* and in the Ohio State edition:[7]

So we passed among the fantastic pillars, till we came to a spot where a number of persons were clustered together, in the light of one of the great stained windows, which seemed to glorify the whole group, as well as the marble that they trod on. Most of them were men of broad foreheads, meditative countenances, and thoughtful, inward eyes; yet it required but a trifle to summon up mirth, peeping out from the very midst of grave and lofty musings. . . . Others stood talking in groups, with a liveliness of expression, a ready smile, and a light, intellectual laughter, which showed how rapidly the shafts of wit were glancing to-and-fro among them.

A few held higher converse, which caused their calm and melancholy souls to beam moonlight from their eyes. As I lingered near them — for I felt an inward attraction towards these men, as if the sympathy of a feeling, if not of genius, had united me to their order — my friend mentioned several of their names. The world has likewise heard those names; with some it has been familiar for years; and others are daily making their way deeper into the universal heart.

"Thank heaven," observed I to my companion, as we passed to another part of the hall, "we have done with this techy, wayward, shy, proud, unreasonable set of laurel-gatherers."

The only proper response to that last paragraph is *"What?"* There is nothing in the *Mosses* or Ohio State text to account for the line about techy, wayward, shy, proud, unreasonable laurel-gatherers. In the *Pioneer* text, however, that line followed an extensive passage in which some much-admired men were named, in which the right of "a number of ladies" to be in the Hall of Fantasy was questioned, and in which, at the end, Rufus Griswold, the anthologizer, was depicted in the act of jotting down the names of poets and poetesses in his memorandum book. To print the *Mosses* version, as the Ohio State Hawthorne does, is to print nonsense under the aegis of respecting an "author's final intention," no matter how arbitrary or ill-conceived. Hawthorne made the cuts, but he did nothing to render the remaining parts of the piece coherent; and what is left is not even *authorial nonsense,* for he could not have thought out and intended all the ludicrousness of the shortened text.

"The Gentle Boy" and "The Hall of Fantasy" are both minor pieces, perhaps, although they might not be perceived as so slight if they were more often anthologized in their original forms. But the same sort of arbitrary textual decisions are made about acknowledged classics, such as *Huckleberry Finn.* Although others had anticipated him in part, Peter G. Beidler was the first to lay out cogently the major textual-critical problems arising from the fact that just before publication Mark Twain decided not to include in *Huckleberry Finn* the long section which we know as the raftsmen's episode or the raft episode.[8] As Beidler showed, it was

Charles Webster, Mark Twain's nephew and publisher, who suggested dropping the episode from the book, apparently to make it nearer the size of *Tom Sawyer.* Mark Twain hastily agreed, without even checking the manuscript or a set of the proofs to see for sure whether any damage would result from the excision. Beidler shows that in fact the deletion left the narrative confused. In Chapter 15 Huck and Jim pass Cairo in the fog, without knowing it. Mark Twain in *Life on the Mississippi* says this, simply as a matter of fact, and the raftsmen's episode confirms it, although it is not something that can readily be learned from the book as published until late in Chapter 16. In the fog Huck and Jim are separated; after the fog lifts Huck finds Jim and plays a mean trick on him, then humbles himself to apologize. Then at the start of Chapter 16 comes the big excision and the consequent illogicalities. As Beidler shows, the text we always read juxtaposes two contradictory paragraphs. In the second paragraph of Chapter 16 Jim and Huck are figuring out how to know Cairo when they see it, not knowing that they have already passed it in the fog. They decide the only thing to do is to paddle ashore the first time they see a light and ask how far it is to Cairo. Yet the third paragraph begins "There warn't nothing to do, now, but to look out sharp for the town, and not to pass it without seeing it." That is, Huck and Jim plan in one paragraph to watch for a light and inquire how far it is to Cairo then in the next paragraph they unaccountably plan to watch for the lights of Cairo itself, since there is no other recourse. Between these paragraphs the raftsmen passage originally stood. As Beidler points out, Huck had gotten into so much trouble by swimming to the raft that he wasn't about to watch for a light in order to query someone else, whether on the river or in an isolated house ashore. The manuscript made perfect sense (and even provided an early clue that Huck and Jim are south of Cairo, since the raftsmen scoff at Huck the moment he speaks of coming *to* Cairo downriver); the published text makes nonsense, if we stop to read it. Yet if the Iowa-California edition appears with the raftsmen's episode as an integral part of the text, there will be enraged protests. Hamlin Hill, for instance, is on record as saying "To add the raftsmen passage to the body of Mark Twain's text is a literary tampering." According to Hill, the passage "belongs out (good or bad) because Mark Twain left it out."[9] Again we see the tyranny of the notion of author's final intention and the failure to analyze the aesthetic implications of "intention."

This textual problem with *Huckleberry Finn* is editorial child's play in comparison with the problems involving *Pudd'nhead Wilson*. To begin with, we have to be clear that what we know as *Pudd'nhead Wilson* is about half the book that Mark Twain completed and tried to publish, using as title for the very large typescript either *Pudd'nhead Wilson* or *Those Extraordinary Twins*, titles now identified with separate publications (still other parts were left unpublished by Mark Twain). The typescript, which Mark Twain had made in Florence in early 1893, was based on the manuscript now in the Morgan Library.[10] The first part in terms of composition was a great mass of material about Angelo and Luigi, bickering Siamese twins. Tom Driscoll was a belated addition, a local white scamp who is heir to the fortune of his uncle, Judge Driscoll. Late in the work on the story of the twins, Mark Twain had a brainstorm: Tom was to be a changeling and murder the judge, who was only thought to be his uncle. At the same time Mark Twain invented Roxana as the slave who had exchanged her baby with her master's. Mark Twain wrote the story of the murder and the trial then went back to write the account of Roxy's exchanging the babies and their growing up. Besides the many pages about the Siamese twins, the manuscript — and the typescript made from it — contained a number of passages not in the published versions of either *Pudd'nhead Wilson* or *Those Extraordinary Twins*, among them some banter between Roxy and Jasper, a fuller account of Roxy's steamboat, the Grand Mogul, and additional pages on Tom's sadism and his broodings over being a part-black bastard. Mark Twain's publisher, Fred Hall, plainly found the work unfit to present to the public. Early in the summer of 1893 Mark Twain decided that he had two stories in one typescript, and extracted most of the material on the twins (that is, most of the pages he had written first), leaving what he had written at the second stage (from about the time Tom sells Roxy down the river to the end) and much (by no means all) of what he wrote last, the early history of Roxy and the children and her revelation to Tom that he is a slave. Mark Twain sold the Roxy-Tom-Pudd'nhead story to the *Century* for serialization as *Pudd'nhead Wilson,* then published it in 1894 as the first part of a volume which also included much of the deleted twins material under the title *Those Extraordinary Twins.*

Significant implications for criticism lie in the evidence about the priority of inscription, but I will not discuss them here other than to point out that anyone is wrong who has ever talked about Mark Twain's sustained interest in slavery in *Pudd'nhead Wilson* or about his loss of interest in Tom, Roxy, or Chambers (the true Tom). Most of the middle of the book was written before slavery was a theme at all, so that we go bathetically from Chapter 10, where Tom is worrying about being part black, to Chapter 11, which was written long before and in which Tom has almost nothing on his limited white mind; and except for the courtroom scenes at the end, when Mark Twain was wholly absorbed in Pudd'nhead's triumph, his interest in Tom and Roxy, and to a large extent in Chambers, grew steadily as he wrote them into his manuscript, although the fact that most of their stronger scenes occur toward the beginning has misled many critics.

The excisions in *Pudd'nhead Wilson* fall into two categories.

Most importantly, of course, the book itself is the product of the excisions of many pages dealing with the Siamese twins. There was no reason to retain the twins in *Pudd'nhead Wilson*, Mark Twain realized, and he kept them in only when taking them out would have required rewriting. His minimal intention was to separate them into ordinary fraternal twins wherever he retained them, but even this plan proved to take more checking than he was willing to give it, and several anomalous references to the twins' being conjoint survived into *Pudd'nhead Wilson*, as various scholars have pointed out.[11]  More subtle effects of the excisions have not been explored, however, such as the consequences for plot and characterization. For instance, in the manuscript the purpose of Tom's going to the Sons of Liberty meeting with the twins was to allow Luigi to kick Tom, thereby leading to elaborate chapters on the legal action Tom brings and the subsequent duel forced upon him by his presumed uncle, during all of which the running joke was first the difficulty of establishing the responsibility for a kick delivered by two men with one pair of legs then the difficulty of arranging a duel in which the cowardly twin would perforce be exposed to danger by the reckless one.  With the twins separated, the kick Luigi delivers to Tom is merely the revenge of a hot-blooded Italian; in the manuscript the revenge had been secondary and the question of which twin did the kicking had been primary.  Tedious as some sobersided readers might find the manuscript scenes in which the twins (or one of them) are (or is) tried for assault, those scenes at least had a coherent purpose.  In the published book, the function of the kicking is diluted almost out of existence.

Besides the grand excisions of scenes involving the twins, Mark Twain also made in the early summer of 1893 still other excisions within the sections he had decided to retain; it is not clear whether or not there were distinct stages of revision, such as first taking the twins out (and taking them apart when they were left in), then making additional cuts in what was left. In any case, the *Pudd'nhead Wilson* which he completed in this revision was further reduced by the loss of pages involving Percy Driscoll's kindness (to white people), Roxy's darky banter with Jasper over theological issues, Roxy's introduction to the splendours of a Mississippi steamboat, many of Tom's ruminations on race and all of his ruminations on bastardy, and an episode in which Tom tortured a grasshopper and two spiders. Mark Twain's avowed purpose, at least in the deletion of the description of the steamboat, was to strip the story for flight,[12] but the effect of these excisions goes far beyond what he implied they would do. Cumulatively the smaller excisions muffle the issue of heredity vs. training and the related issue of whether behaviour traits can be racial in origin. If those cuts involving Roxy tend to leave her portrait as more powerful, though smaller, those involving Tom leave him less intelligent and far less interesting in his malignity.

Curiously enough, Mark Twain's deletion of some of Tom's more complex thoughts works to the good of the book, for one effect, whether intended or not, is that Tom is not exalted quite so high in his ruminations before being brought low in those passages which follow in the published book but which were in fact written earlier, at a time when Tom was a very simple character indeed. To talk about Mark Twain's intentions in regard to *Pudd'nhead Wilson* is to risk absurdity at every word. His intentions shifted erratically, again and again, and many of the most obvious literary effects of the published book — such as its vacillating charac- terizations — are inadvertent, a result of the author's shifting conceptions and hasty excising and splicing together, not part of a genuine artistic intention at all.

By contrast, when one turns to Stephen Crane, the famous case of 1893 *Maggie* vs. 1896 *Maggie* looks simple. In 1955 R. W. Stallman pointed out that the Appleton edition of 1896 was a severe expurgation which omitted, among other words, phrases, and passages, the "fat man" paragraph, the next to last paragraph of Chapter 17 in the original edition:

> When almost to the river the girl saw a great figure. On going forward she perceived it to be a huge fat man in torn and greasy garments. His grey hair straggled down over his forehead. His small, bleared eyes, sparkling from amidst great rolls of red fat, swept eagerly over the girl's upturned face. He laughed, his brown, disordered teeth gleaming under a grey, grizzled moustache from which beer-drops dripped. His whole body gently quivered and shook like that of a dead jelly fish. Chuckling and leering, he followed the girl of the crimson legions.

In the short final paragraph of the chapter in the 1893 edition, Maggie and the fat man stand together in the darkness: "At their feet, the river appeared a deathly black hue. Some hidden factory sent up a yellow glare, that lit for a moment the waters lapping oilily against timbers. The varied sounds of life, made joyous by distance and seeming unapproachableness, came faintly and died away to a silence." Since almost everyone but Fredson Bowers agrees that the 1893 edition is the one we ought to be reading, I am not going to argue the matter here.[13] I just want to make two points.

First, the fat man has a more complicated function in the book as a whole than critics have noticed, although various people have commented on Crane's playing him off against the stout clergyman whom Maggie encounters at the end of Chapter 16. The pattern of Maggie's experience with fat, red people who have dishevelled hair runs all through the book, and includes the small fat man who leers or smiles and bobs his shock of red wig in Chapter 7, Maggie's boss at the collar

and cuff factory in Chapter 8, and, most important, her
mother, that large woman with massive shoulders, huge arms,
huge back, and (in her later years) grey hair that falls in
knotted masses, is tangled, and straggles, "giving her crimson
features a look of insanity." She is Maggie's red mother, and
has red fists as well as a red, writhing body. Even at the level
of paralleling his characters, Crane was doing something more
ambitious and complex than we have recognized. The fat
man is a climactic figure in relation to other, earlier charac-
terizations, as well as in relation to Maggie's descent and
death.

My second point is that we have fallen into the trap of
talking about the ending of Chapter 17 in the Appleton
edition as if it meant something, as if it were part of a distinct
authorial version of the novel. Ripley Hitchcock, the editor
at Appleton's, was dictating the kinds of changes Crane was
making, even if he was not making some of them by himself.
The concern was only to cut the book so that it would *not*
mean what it had plainly meant in the 1893 edition. No one
reconceived the chapter so as to make it have a meaning. In
fact, it was so carelessly cut down that even Bowers admits
that one substituted pronoun cannot make any clear sense.[14]
Because the Appleton text leaves no coherent motivations for
Maggie's actions after deliberately disguising her original
motives and actions, it has proved open to speculation that
her purpose in Chapter 17 is to drown herself, even though
the 1896 text does *not* place her at the river, as the 1893 text
graphically does. Crane never says how Maggie dies. The
idea that she commits suicide is not authorial but adventitious,
projected by sense-making readers onto the quite literally
unintelligible 1896 text. There are not two authorial versions
of *Maggie* in anything like the sense that there are two versions of James's *The American*. The conditions under which
the expurgation was conducted were such as to prohibit
Crane from reconceiving the book, even if he were the sort of

writer who liked to revise his published works. To argue that Crane was expurgating with one hand and incorporating many artistic revisions with the other, as Fredson Bowers does, is to ignore the biographical and textual evidence: you don't add your final artistic flourishes to something you are wrecking because you are being forced to expurgate it painfully, line by line.[15]   In his eagerness to follow author's final intentions Bowers has followed Ripley Hitchcock's intentions, not Crane's.

I have always avoided teaching *The Red Badge of Courage* whenever I could substitute something else by Crane that made sense, such as "The Blue Hotel" or "The Monster." When I did teach it I often used William M. Gibson's Rinehart Edition, so that at least when there is no "conviction" in the Appleton text — at the point where we are told "With this conviction came a store of assurance" — I could point to the bracketed words from the manuscript to show what Crane had meant.   Three years ago Brian Higgins and I wrote a long essay on the Virginia *Maggie* and for the March 1976 *Nineteenth-Century Fiction* I wrote a review of the Virginia *Red Badge* and the NCR Microcards Facsimile of *Red Badge,* both edited by Fredson Bowers.  At first I was distracted because there were so many things wrong with the Virginia *Red Badge,* but at last I realized that the same familiar pattern of expurgation was working in *Red Badge* that worked a few months later in *Maggie:*  to Ripley Hitchcock's eyes, the manuscript of *Red Badge* was blasphemous and a commercial liability.  I decided that we ought to be reading what Crane wrote rather than what Appleton printed, and laid out in the review how we could recover almost all of what Crane wrote — you just put back in the surviving pages of the original Chapter 12 (eked out by passages from the rough draft), include all the x'd out passages at the ends of chapters, include all the passages which were *not* x'd out but which nevertheless did not appear in the Appleton edition, and whenever possible, as in Chapter 12, supply the substance of a missing passage from a surviving passage of the rough draft. I wagered, in the review, that such a reconstruction of the manuscript would be "the best possible basis for New Critical demonstrations of the unity of the novel — the sort of essays which have been lavished upon mere reprints (or reprints of reprints) of the Appleton text, a text which reached its final form as the result of omissions so hasty and ill-conceived that several passages still depend for their meaning upon passages which were excised."

Since then Henry Binder, a former student of mine, has edited the manuscript and read it. He has also turned up previously unknown documents, including the letter in which Hitchcock accepted *The Third Violet* while specifying the sort of changes he wished Crane would make in it. Binder has now established the pattern of Hitchcock's intervention in all four of the Crane books he edited — including, in a minor way, *The Little Regiment.* More importantly, Binder has shown that *The Red Badge of Courage* is an astonishingly different and better book than the one Appleton printed and we have always read. Among other things, he has established that the manuscript was a much more ambitious psychological study than what Appleton published, and was far more coherent than any critic of Crane has been able to claim on the basis of the maimed Appleton text. What I give is only a brief preview of one of Binder's findings, but enough to give some sense of the consequences of Hitchcock's concern to print a novel in which the twerp of the opening chapters did not remain a twerp but became a man.[16]

In the original Chapter 15, the day after the first battle, the matured loud soldier, here called merely the friend or Wilson, breaks up a quarrel, only to have the quarrellers turn on him. As Wilson tells Henry Fleming, "Jimmie Rogers ses I'll have t' fight him after th' battle t'-day. . . . He ses he don't allow no interferin' in his business. I hate t' see th' boys fightin' 'mong themselves." The next time Jimmie Rogers is mentioned is in Chapter 19. He is shot through the body and raising a cry of bitter lamentation. Wilson gets permission to go and get water for Jimmie Rogers and Henry goes along — not out of concern for Jimmie Rogers but merely because he feels a desire to throw his heated body into the stream and, soaking there, drink quarts. In the Appleton edition, that's all — no more Jimmie Rogers. Crane critics have talked about animals and suns and wafers and much more, but not about Jimmie Rogers, who in the Appleton text is last heard screaming on the battlefield. Yet what Binder shows is that Crane was building very painstakingly toward the climactic third mention of Jimmie Rogers as a way of emphasizing, in the last chapter, that Henry Fleming has not grown into anything like Wilson's mature selflessness. In the last chapter, as Crane wrote it, Wilson has a sudden, confused thought:

> "Good Lord!" repeated his friend. "Yeh know Jimmie Rogers? Well, he — gosh, when he was hurt I started t'get some water fer 'im an', thunder, I aint seen 'im from that time 'til this. I clean forgot what I — say, has anybody seen Jimmie Rogers?"
> "Seen 'im? No! He's dead," they told him.
> His friend swore.
> But the youth, regarding his procession of memory, felt gleeful and unregretting, for, in it, his public deeds were paraded in great and shining prominence. Those performances which had been witnessed by his fellows marched now in wide purple and gold, hiding various deflections. They went gaily, with music. It was pleasure to watch these things. He spent delightful minutes viewing the gilded images of memory.

This was all censored out. It was not blasphemous, like some of the earlier chapter endings, all of the original Chapter 12, and parts of the ending of the last chapter, and it was not profane, like much of *Maggie*, but it was not heroic and it was not nice. It depicted a psychological process which was too distastefully selfish and vainglorious to appear with the Appleton imprint when a few cuts here and there would let readers come to the conclusion that, somehow, Henry Fleming had become a man.

The use of Jimmie Rogers is only one example of the ways in which Binder shows the Appleton edition to have destroyed Crane's intended meanings by repeated excising and splicing together. The present controversy among the critics over the meaning of *The Red Badge of Courage* would not have arisen if Hitchcock had printed what Crane wrote. You can't guarantee that critics would not have found other grounds for spurious quarrels, but everyone would have known that Henry Fleming did not become a man. Once again textual scholars have blindly obeyed what they took to be the author's final intentions. Not seeing any pattern to Hitchcock's editing, Fredson Bowers in the Virginia Edition printed a very heavily and erratically emended version of the Appleton text, by far the most confused text of *Red Badge* ever printed, but firm in its preference for the Appleton excisions.[17] In the new Norton Critical Edition Donald Pizer says firmly: "we should permit Crane the last word — that of the Appleton text — and not attempt to return the novel to a state which he had rejected or revised in the course of composition."[18] Joseph Katz has been perhaps the most dogmatic about the primacy of the Appleton edition. In *Proof* he says: "there is one authoritative source of the text: the first edition. Simple."[19] In the Viking Portable he says: "One must conclude that most of the omitted manuscript readings do not appear in the published novel because Crane did not want them there. To include them in a reading text, even though they are distinguished by typographical devices from those portions of the novel taken from the first edition, is to ask a reader to absorb a work that was never meant to exist."[20] What Katz says here is even more perplexing than it may sound at first. He says that the manuscript version of *Red Badge* "was never meant to exist." Of course it was meant to exist. It *existed,* and it is what Crane peddled about New York in 1894 and what he offered to Appleton's after whetting Hitchcock's appetite with clippings from the martial newspaper condensation. At that time Crane remarked that the manuscript version was the original one and better by far than the newspaper one, in his mind. Except in the commercial sense that Crane agreed to changes in order to have the book published (after he had all but given up hope of placing it), the manuscript version which he completed in 1894 and finished polishing while at New Orleans in March 1895 is the *only* form of the text that Crane meant to exist.

Statements from leading textual experts like those I have cited close off textual study in arbitrary obedience to Greg (or what the experts think Greg would have wanted). Again and again mechanical application of Greg has allowed scholars to ignore bibliographical, historical, and biographical evidence that should have been brought to bear on the text. Nor have scholars in related disciplines been very helpful. When I see people in psycholinguistics conducting their experiments in what happens to comprehension when a CLUCK is introduced at various points in an English sentence, I begin to wish they would come over into the textual field. There is already a great mass of data available to them in the apparatuses of the CEAA editions which, taken together with contemporary reviews and later criticism of works which have been known in problematical texts, constitutes invaluable evidence as to how real readers have made sense of the cryptic or illogical or nonsensical, or — more rarely — have recognized that texts were flawed.

For all that has been written on author's final intention, or simply on "intention," we have precisely *one* attempt to deal with the concept in a way that reconciles editorial terminology with that of literary theory, speech-act theory, and psycholinguistics. I mean G. Thomas Tanselle's awesome essay on "The Editorial Problem of Final Authorial Intention."[21] The essay is perhaps most vulnerable at those points where Tanselle adopts Michael Hancher's distinctions among three kinds of intention, none of which has specifically to do with the writer's shifting intentions during the actual process of writing and during any stages of revision, whether before or after "completion" and publication. What we need are more studies like Tanselle's — studies which work carefully with many complex textual situations and are of a sophistication (in literary theory as well as textual theory) that would make them publishable not just in *Studies in Bibliography, Papers of the Bibliographical Society of America,* and *Proof,* but also in *New Literary History* and *Critical Inquiry.* Textual scholars need to educate, and be educated by, aestheticians, speech-act theorists, and students of creativity theory, among others. Information is available in an abundance unthinkable twenty years ago. Now it is time to start thinking about what that information means. For the present, a good many textual editors seem almost paralyzed by elementary difficulties such as those involved in authorial excisions: Greg has been used too long as a bulwark against thought about this particular textual problem.

NOTES

1  W. W. Greg, "The Rationale of Copy-Text," *Studies in Bibliography,* 3 (1950-51), 19-36.

2  "Bibliography and the Novelistic Fallacy," *Studies in Bibliography,* 12 (1959), 59-73.

3   "The First Two Volumes of *The Writing of Henry D. Thoreau:* A Review Article," *Proof* 4 (1975), 215-35. Although I am suggesting that Thoreau made the pre-publication excisions and made them for good reasons, I am not challenging McElrath's important speculation that the last stage of the manuscript should be copy-text rather than the proofs or the first edition, since Thoreau's manuscript punctuation and spelling was greatly altered in proofs and not significantly restored in the first edition.

4   *The Annotated Walden,* ed. Philip Van Doren Stern, New York, Clarkson N. Potter, 1970; many of Stern's quotations from the various stages of the manuscript derive from F. B. Sanborn's edition of *Walden,* Boston, Bibliophile Society, 1909.

5   Nathaniel Hawthorne, *Twice-Told Tales,* Columbus, Ohio State University Press, 1974, p. 547, and *Mosses from an Old Manse,* Columbus, Ohio State University Press, 1974, p. 556.

6   From Hawthorne's prefatory comments in *The Gentle Boy: A Thrice Told Tale,* Boston, Weeks, Jordan, 1839.

7   *Mosses from an Old Manse,* p. 175. The excised passages are printed only in the "Historical Collation," pp. 634-39, although they are surely the parts of the sketch which have most enduring interest. Good use is made of the original version in Buford Jones, " 'The Hall of Fantasy' and the Early Hawthorne-Thoreau Relationship," PMLA, 83 (1968), 1429-38.

8   Peter G. Beidler, "The Raft Episode in *Huckleberry Finn,*" *Modern Fiction Studies,* 14 (1968), 11-20.

9   See Hill's introduction to his photo-facsimile of the first edition of *Huckleberry Finn,* San Francisco, Chandler, 1962, p. xii.

10   The following comments on *Pudd'nhead Wilson* derive from my work on the forthcoming Iowa-California Edition. In some examples I have profited from my student Philip Cohen's eagle eye for a textually-caused aesthetic anomaly.

11   The first to enumerate the anomalies was George W. Feinstein, "Vestigia in *Pudd'nhead Wilson,*" *The Twainian,* 1 (1942), 1-3.

12   *Mark Twain's Letters to his Publishers: 1867-1894,* ed. Hamlin Hill,

Berkeley, University of California Press, 1967, p. 355: "I have knocked out everything that delayed the march of the story – even the description of a Mississippi steamboat. There ain't any weather in, and there ain't any scenery – the story is stripped for flight!"

13  For one example, see Donald Pizer, review of the first two volumes of the Virginia Edition of Stephen Crane, *Modern Philology,* 68 (1970), 212-14.

14  *Bowery Tales,* ed. Fredson Bowers, Charlottesville, University Press of Virginia, 1969, pp. lxxxix-xc.

15  See *Bowery Tales*, pp. lxvi-lxxiii and elsewhere.

16  Binder's "*The Red Badge of Courage* Nobody Knows" will appear in a special Stephen Crane number of *Studies in the Novel.*

17  *The Red Badge of Courage,* ed. Fredson Bowers, Charlottesville, University Press of Virginia, 1975. p. 234: "The cuts in the A1 [Appleton] text, as well as its few additions, are taken to be authoritative."

18  *The Red Badge of Courage,* Second Edition, New York. W. W. Norton, 1976, "A Note on the Text," p. 3: "In short, except for obvious errors which occurred in the transmission of the text from the manuscript to the typescript to print, we should permit Crane the last word – that of the Appleton text – and not attempt to return the novel to a state which he had rejected or revised in the course of composition."

19  "Practical Editions: Stephen Crane's *The Red Badge of Courage*," *Proof,* 2 (1972), 303.

20  *The Portable Stephen Crane,* New York, Viking Press, 1969, p. xxii.

21  *Studies in Bibliography,* 29 (1976), 167-211.

# Members of the Conference

Peter Allen, *University of Toronto*
Henry Auster, *University of Toronto*
Roberta Buchanan, *Memorial University of Newfoundland*
Michael Collie, *York University*
Don L. Cook, *Indiana University*
Rose C. D'Agostino, *State University of New York, Albany*
J. A. Dainard, *University of Toronto*
A. H. de Quehen, *University of Toronto*
Susan Dick, *Queen's University*
Eric Domville, *University of Toronto*
J. Peter Dyson, *University of Toronto*
Donald D. Eddy, *Cornell University*
David V. Erdman, *State University of New York, Stony Brook, and New York Public Library*
A. Graham Falconer, *University of Toronto*
George H. Ford, *University of Rochester*

Hilda Gifford, *Carleton University*
H. K. Girling, *York University*
Joseph Gold, *University of Waterloo*
Ila Goody, *University of Toronto*
Judith Grant, *University of Guelph*
Francess G. Halpenny, *University of Toronto*
Edgar F. Harden, *Simon Fraser University*
Bruce Harkness, *Kent State University*
Patricia Hernlund, *Wayne State University*
Elizabeth Hulse, *University of Toronto*
J. R. de J. Jackson, *University of Toronto*
Jean C. Jamieson, *University of Toronto Press*
Richard C. Johnson, *Newberry Library*
Dale Kramer, *University of Illinois, Urbana-Champaign*
Michael Laine, *University of Toronto*
Anne Lancashire, *University of Toronto*
Richard G. Landon, *University of Toronto*
Roger C. Lewis, *Acadia University*
Douglas G. Lochhead, *Mount Allison University*
Bruce R. Lundgren, *University of Western Ontario*
Juliet McMaster, *University of Alberta*
R. D. McMaster, *University of Alberta*
T. G. Middlebro', *Carleton University*
Jane Millgate, *University of Toronto*
Michael Millgate, *University of Toronto*
Sylvère Monod, *University of Paris-III (Sorbonne)*
Eugene F. Murphy, *Hobart and William Smith Colleges*
Irena Murray, *McGill University*
Desmond Neill, *University of Toronto*
Robert O'Kell, *University of Manitoba*
Andrew Oliver, *University of Toronto*
Dorothy Parker, *University of Toronto*
Hershel Parker, *University of Southern California*
Anne C. Pilgrim, *York University*
A. William Plumstead, *Laurentian University*

S. W. Reid, *Kent State University*
F. Warren Roberts, *University of Texas, Austin*
C. E. Sanborn, *University of Western Ontario*
Robert C. Schweik, *State University of New York, Fredonia*
G. B. Shand, *York University*
Peter L. Shillingsburg, *Mississippi State University*
Reginald C. Terry, *University of Victoria*
Clive Thomson, *University of Toronto*
Vincent L. Tollers, *State University of New York, Brockport*
Prudence Tracy, *University of Toronto Press*
Elizabeth Waterston, *University of Guelph*
Edgar Wright, *Laurentian University*
Janet Wright, *University of Toronto*
Dorothy Zaborszky, *Laurentian University*
George J. Zytaruk, *Nipissing University College*

# Index

## Date Due

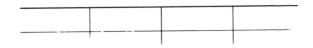